THE UNIVERSITY OF
WINCHESTER

Martial Rose Library
Tel: 01962 827306

To be returned on or before the day marked above,

D1345603

mistic answer: "We would be happier without vanity. Nevertheless we cannot do anything about it."

The thesis of the essay is that vanity is an innate human trait but one that has been become more and more pronounced over many generations for two reasons. One is that the repeated experience of gaining benefits from the approval of others gives rise to habits of behavior that persist even in situations where no such advantage is at hand. The other explanation runs along Darwinian lines: the impulse to seek the approval of others is an innate trait that has increased over many generations because of natural selection. Vanity provides an advantage for the individual in the struggle for existence, since the good opinion of others, even if it does not bring immediate benefit, is likely to be of use on other occasions. These two arguments are closely linked, for Rée is assuming that the habits individuals acquire, especially in their early lives, have some tendency to be passed on to their descendants as innate qualities. The heritability of acquired characteristics is a concept usually associated with Lamarck, but it is also present to some extent in Darwin, who writes, "I think it can be shown that this does sometimes happen."[21] Rée's overall argument is thus that continual reinforcement of an inborn tendency toward vanity has combined with natural selection to bring about a dominating influence on human behavior as we now see it.

The link with Darwin goes beyond a simple appeal to these theoretical ideas. Rée cites Darwin's treatment of animal behavior in his essay on sexual selection as a main source for the "Essay on Vanity." There, Darwin argues that many animals have acquired a drive to behavior that can be explained only as an impulse to gain the admiration of others for the purpose of mating, but which is often seen apart from that situation. Sexual selection is especially noticeable in birds: their songs, dances, and displays of plumage are all developed for courtship. "But nothing is more common than for animals to take pleasure in practicing whatever instinct they follow at other times for some real purpose," Darwin adds.[22] He applies the model of sexual selection to human beings only with reference to characteristics such as hair and skin color. Yet given the fact that, like natural selection in general, the principle applies just as much to instincts as to physical features in the case of other species, Rée's argument about human beings suggests itself as a plausible extension of the Darwinian theory.

The discussion of vanity in *Psychological Observations* may be seen as a first sketch for the more ambitious theorizing of *The Origin of the Moral Sensations.* The most obvious overlap between the two works is seen in the chapter on vanity in *The Origin of the Moral Sensations,* which, as Rée states in a footnote, reuses some of the earlier material. But the treatment of the book's central theme, the phenomenon of unselfishness and its moral interpretation, is also closely parallel in its structure. Again, a moral quality is identified as problematical for theoretical understanding, a naturalistic account is offered in its explanation, and the question of its contribution to human happiness is raised at the end, only to be given a generally pessimistic answer.

Rée begins by characterizing his strategy as that of a scientist who first observes and then tries to account for some natural phenomenon. His choice of the geologist as an example is significant, given that one of the important scientific developments of the nineteenth century—and a contributing factor in the emergence of the theory of evolution—was the geological theory that postulated processes of development occurring long before recorded history. However, it would be truer to say that Rée's primary model is Schopenhauer's essay *On the Basis of Morality*. Like Rée, Schopenhauer states his program by denying that his ethics will have any imperative force. His aim is not to tell people how they *ought* to behave:

> I assume, on the other hand, that the purpose of ethics is to indicate, explain and trace to its ultimate ground the extremely varied behavior of men from a moral point of view. Therefore there is no other way for discovering the foundation of ethics than the empirical, namely, to investigate whether there are generally any actions to which we must ascribe genuine moral worth. Such will be actions of voluntary justice, pure philanthropy, and real magnanimity. These are then to be regarded as a given phenomenon that we have to explain correctly, that is, trace to its true grounds.[23]

Schopenhauer's answer is that morality rests on a feeling of compassion that occurs naturally and which alone is the source of those actions we judge as worthy of moral approval. His discussion begins with a lengthy critique of Kant's formalistic theory of morality, an approach that abstracts entirely from natural feelings such as benevolence and sympathy. Kant holds that moral behavior can be motivated solely by respect for the moral law and that this is indeed its only possible motivation. Schopenhauer's main objection to this doctrine is that it fails to supply any empirical motive that could act as an influence strong enough to overcome the selfish feelings and passions that dominate human nature. The notion that reason alone can be sufficient is, he argues, a delusion. A real motive can be opposed successfully only by another, stronger real motive; and rational insight provides nothing of that kind. A second line of criticism is that Kant's presentation of a moral law in imperative form is a mistake. According to Schopenhauer, the vocabulary of "law" and "duty" is a hangover from the "theological morals" typified by the Ten Commandments. In any case, he adds, the concept of obligation remains bound up with reward and punishment and is thus, in the end, an appeal to self-interest rather than an expression of morality.

After this, the essay turns to what Schopenhauer calls the "skeptical view," that there is really *no* inner basis for morality, that it consists only in human customs designed to avoid conflict and promote the benefit of individuals and groups. Observation of human nature confirms that much of what passes for morality is in fact determined by social influences, such as the threat of punishment or the power of public opinion. The question is whether such explanations cover *all* instances of moral behavior. Schopenhauer argues that some actions cannot be accounted for in this way: for instance, acts of justice, of charity, and especially of self-sacrifice. It is true that we cannot appeal directly to experience for confirmation of this claim, since the outward action is observed, but not the motive behind it. Yet the fact that we have a sense of morality at all gives strong support to the belief in such actions, for the only criterion of moral worth is the lack of self-interest that we identify in them. If unselfishness were impossible, morality would be a mere illusion.[24]

Only at the end of *On the Basis of Morality* does Schopenhauer go further and touch on the conditions under which these selfless feelings or motives can exist. He argues that what is essential to the moral person is "that he makes less of a distinction than do the rest between himself and others."[25] Is this a genuine insight or simply a mistake? It cannot be justified by empirical considerations: "According to experience, the *difference* between my person and another's appears to be absolute." However, Kant has demonstrated that empirical knowledge is directed only toward phenomena, which are conditioned by our own forms of intuition, space, and time, rather than toward things as they are in themselves. In that case, plurality and separateness are only features of appearances, and the ancient tradition that speaks of an underlying unity of all things represents a wisdom that, Schopenhauer suggests, is embodied in every morally praiseworthy action.

The task that Rée sets himself in *The Origin of the Moral Sensations* goes further still. For he accepts Schopenhauer's answer to the question about the basis of morality, but not his further speculation. That is, Rée too traces all morally praiseworthy behavior back to selfless motives, but offers a naturalistic rather than a metaphysical explanation for the existence of such feelings by calling on the Darwinian theory of evolution through natural selection. He then raises the question: how have these motives, and the actions arising from them, come to be understood as *morality*? This is where Rée wanted to advance beyond the existing Darwinian approach. Selfless behavior is observed in other species, but only in human beings is it *interpreted* in this particular way. Darwin plays down such differences, but Rée thinks it is important to recognize the specificity of moral thinking. Morality is not a straightforward expression of feelings, but a conceptual construction that builds in features of both individual and social development. The outcome is "conscience," a phenomenon that Rée takes not to be present in other species, even those that do exhibit non-egoistic traits. The conceptualization of non-egoistic behavior as morally good depends on associations of ideas, habits of behavior, and social conventions. Although what makes an action good or bad is just its beneficial or harmful effects on others, these processes make goodness or badness *seem* to be qualities of the act, taken by itself. Hence, Rée concludes, there is a kind of systematic illusion involved in morality. As he puts it, we forget that "good" originally means good *for* something—that is, *useful*—and take it to be an intrinsic property of motives and actions. Yet, given the usual pattern of human development, this impression is a natural and inescapable one.

The illusory character of moral concepts is especially evident in the case of justice, where the transformation of utility into moral goodness and badness is brought about through the practice of punishment—a subject that comes to dominate Rée's thinking about morality after *The Origin of the Moral Sensations.* Society finds it useful to control the behavior of its members by enforcing rules and laws by means of sanctions. The purpose of legal punishment is to deter future offences, but when it is inflicted, that aim is not manifest in the procedures followed by the authorities. Hence, the impression is given of a *direct* relationship between wrongdoing and liability to punishment. The feeling that corresponds to this association of ideas is the "sense of justice." As he does with moral thinking in general, Rée cites the typical experiences of childhood as evidence in support of his account. Children are told "You are punished because you have done this," rather than "You are punished so that you will not do this again." As a result, they acquire the notion of *retribution,* that is, a seemingly immediate relation between wrongdoing and liability to punishment. This becomes a powerful presence in moral thinking, especially when it is associated with the notion of free will.

Rée's moral psychology is close to that of Herbert Spencer, who similarly relies on the concepts of habit and association in supplying a naturalistic explanation of the moral sensations. Spencer's general account is best summarized in an open letter to John Stuart Mill, quoted in Darwin's *Descent of Man,* where he writes, "I believe that the experiences of utility organized and consolidated through all past generations of the human race, have been producing corresponding modifications, which, by continued transmission and improvement, have become in us certain faculties of moral intuition—certain emotions responding to right and wrong conduct, which have no apparent basis in the individual experiences of utility."[26] The task of moral science, Spencer argues, is to refine and systematize the "rough conclusions" that arise from these intuitions, in much the same way that the science of geometry starts with spatial feelings but arrives at theorems whose validity is independent of empirical experience.[27] The necessary truth of geometric propositions shows that they are not just empirical generalizations arrived at through induction from some diverse range of experiences. Spencer claims a similar status for his own science of "absolute" or "rational" ethics and repeatedly asserts that its propositions are necessary and universal truths for which there is not even a coherent alternative. "Thus," he typically writes, "the ultimate development of the ideal man is logically certain."[28]

This thesis signals a crucial difference between Spencer's evolutionism and Darwin's. For Spencer, evolution is synonymous with progress. He believes in a universal law of development, consisting in a continual growth of complexity, or "the transformation of the homogeneous into the heterogeneous."[29] This model is postulated as existing everywhere in nature, even within the inorganic world, for example, in the origin of the solar system. In the living world, it is seen in the growth and development of individual organisms. And for humanity as a whole, the advance of society from a primitive to a civilized state is regarded by Spencer as a necessary process, guaranteed by the universal principle of development, from which one can predict the future rise of humanity to a state of "perfection."

Spencer's use of the word "evolution," established before the appearance of Darwin's theory, always carries with it this sense of progress—a usage which has given rise to endless misconceptions about Darwin's quite different theory. Darwin tended to avoid the expression "evolution" for this reason and, in a similar way, was wary of referring to different forms of life as "higher" or "lower."[30] He seems to have foreseen the kind of identification of his scientific theory with Spencer's doctrine that has, in fact, commonly occurred ever since. On the Darwinian view, it must be emphasized, there is no natural tendency to greater complexity, as postulated by Lamarck and Spencer. It may well be that a more complex form is favored by natural selection, but the same mechanism can lead toward simplification in other situations. In any case, the economical nature of the theory of natural selection—a primary reason for its appeal—would be compromised by the addition of an independent principle of explanation such as Spencer's "law of progress."

This belief in a continual advance of humanity toward the ideal is certainly not shared by Rée. A whole chapter of *The Origin of the Moral Sensations* is devoted to attacking the doctrine of moral progress. Rée's strategy is to run through the possible mechanisms that might bring about a general moral improvement and eliminate each one in turn. Natural selection, he argues, has no tendency to increase the number of selfless people, for such individuals are at a disadvantage compared to others and have fewer prospects of surviving or leaving descendants. And further, it is true that, as Darwin argued in *The Descent of Man,* a tribe that displays strong mutual loyalty will have an advantage in competition with other tribes, but Rée discounts this as an obsolete phenomenon. Modern societies have ways of achieving a stable organization other than reliance upon public feeling: "Selflessness and patriotism are no longer so necessary even in war, now that ambition and the sense of honor render just as good service."

As for the power of habit to alter human character, in accordance with the Lamarckian principle of inheritance of acquired traits, Rée argues that working for others over a long period will have this effect only if it is done purely for others' sake. Most of those who work for the public benefit (such as physicians) act from quite different motives, he argues, often very selfish ones, and so their behavior has no tendency to increase the occurrence of non-egoistic feelings. At most, Rée concludes, moral progress can consist in a certain growth in the human power of self-control. As he puts it, "Human beings become more domesticated with time." This picture is in sharp contrast with Spencer's vision of inevitable social progress toward an enlightened egoism that is consistent with respect for the interests of other people.

After a chapter on vanity that returns to the themes, and even to the aphoristic style, of his earlier book, Rée concludes *The Origin of the Moral Sensations* by raising two further issues concerning morality. The first is this question of moral progress. He is prepared to argue that the process of natural selection and the power of social custom, acting together over a long period, do promote a general increase in non-egoism, although conceding that historical events can cause sharp fluctuations in the moral standards of particular societies. Yet the prevailing pessimism of *Psychological Observations* reappears in full force in the final chapter, which addresses the relation between goodness and happiness. According to Schopenhauer, Kant's great service to ethics had been to "purge" it of eudemonism: that is, of the belief, prevalent among the ancient philosophers, that virtue and happiness are either the same thing, or at least necessarily bound together.[31] Perhaps Rée feels that his theory allows for some reappearance of eudemonism, given that it locates both morality and happiness in the natural realm, in contrast with their metaphysical distinctness in Kant and Schopenhauer. Starting from his premises, he could have ended with the complacent—and indeed, somewhat philistine—picture of the moral life drawn by Herbert Spencer in *The Data of Ethics,* pub-

point of reference for Rée at this stage.[20] The theme running through the work is the prevalence of hidden motives in human action and the hypocrisy of most claims to moral virtue. The most obvious model for Rée's aphoristic style is La Rochefoucauld, whom he plainly admires not only for his mastery of that literary form but also for his uncompromising assessment of human nature. In one section, Rée takes issue with Vauvenargues, who had raised a moral version of the "liar" paradox: if La Rochefoucauld's condemnation of humanity is taken at face value, must it not apply to himself? And in that case, would we be right to respect his judgment? Rée replies, "This question is absurd: for what La Rochefoucauld's followers admire is not the goodness of his heart, but the subtlety of his head." His own opening motto makes a parallel statement about the purpose of his work: "Some read to improve their hearts, others to improve their minds: I write for the latter."

The quality of Rée's aphorisms is variable, but many stand up reasonably well against the high standard he has set for himself, even if, in some cases, one can make an educated guess as to the reflection of La Rochefoucauld or Schopenhauer that has inspired his train of thought. More serious is the fact that, despite the attempted misdirection of the *Nachlass* attribution, implying the author's death and thus suggesting the accumulated knowledge of a full lifetime, the observations often give away the youth of an author who was still in his early twenties. This difference between Rée and his French models comes through especially clearly in certain areas. When La Rochefoucauld writes of the pain of jealousy, the disappointments of life, and the prospect of death, it is with a voice of experience that cannot be found in Rée. In place of such hard-won understanding, his "psychological observations" fall back on a rather facile and cynical worldly wisdom, although this works well enough when applied to superficial aspects of social life and manners.

The "Essay on Vanity" that concludes *Psychological Observations* is an exercise in a very different style of writing. Vanity had been a frequent theme in the previous part of the book, and yet it comes as a surprise to go from those short and sharp observations to an extended argument about a wide range of human behavior. Rée gives the word "vanity" [*Eitelkeit*] a broadened sense, although the impact of his formulations often relies on the reader's having the narrower sense in mind. For Rée "vanity" means any pleasure taken in the good opinion of others and pain caused by their bad opinion, apart from the further consequences that such opinions might have. The essay interprets other moral qualities, such as the sense of honor, as variants on this theme. Having argued for the prevalence of vanity in human nature, Rée finally raises the question whether vanity makes us happier, and he gives a thoroughly pessi-

Catastrophic though this experience may have been for Nietzsche, it did little harm to the close relationship between Rée and Lou. Now established in Berlin, they continued to live and travel together for four more years. In 1883 they formed a new "trio" by bringing another person with them on a trip to Switzerland: the young Ferdinand Tönnies, later to become a leading authority in sociology and author of one of the few published reviews of Rée's life and work. Two years later, a similar arrangement was made, this time with Max Heinemann, a Berlin attorney and admirer of Lou, whose first novel, *Im Kampf um Gott,* [In the struggle for God] was causing a stir among the German reading public. However, whatever plans Rée may still have had to set up a "monastery" of free spirits came to nothing in the face of a new development. In 1886 Lou announced her decision to marry a Persian scholar, Friedrich Carl Andreas. Rée withdrew in agitated haste, perceiving that his position in such a configuration could only be the outer one that Nietzsche had occupied. Lou entered into a typically unconventional marriage with Andreas, and when he was appointed as professor in Göttingen, she moved there permanently.

Rée's life had in any case taken a new course in 1885. He published his long-planned work on the origin of conscience, as well as a short essay on free will, the last productions to appear during his lifetime. Having abandoned his attempts to gain a position in a German university, he began studying medicine in Berlin and then Zurich, qualifying as a medical practitioner in Munich in 1890. For nearly ten years, Rée worked as a country physician on the family estate, where his reputation for selfless service would have surprised readers of *Psychological Observations.* When his older brother Georg Rée sold the property and retired to Berlin in 1900, the secure basis on which Rée had always built his life was removed. He wandered back to Switzerland, retracing his old steps. By the autumn of 1901, he had been staying for more than a year at the hotel Misani in Celerina—the same place that he and Lou had visited on their last trips together. On 28 October 1901 Rée died under slightly obscure circumstances after falling from a mountain path overlooking the Inn River. A Swiss police investigation returned a finding of accidental death, but speculation has continued and the nature of his death is unlikely to be settled.

TOWARD A NATURAL HISTORY OF MORALITY

Rée's first book was published anonymously in 1875 under the title *Psychologische Beobachtungen: Aus dem Nachlass von ***.* This compact volume of 158 pages contains 475 aphorisms arranged under various headings, followed by a short essay on vanity.[19] Its general tone is set by a motto on the title page, *L'homme est l'animal méchant par excellence* [Man is the wickedest of all animals], a line taken from Gobineau, most likely by way of Schopenhauer, a main

posed in the photographic studio of Jules Bonnet for a now-famous picture showing Rée and Nietzsche tethered to a cart in which Lou sits, wielding a whip. She later stated that Nietzsche had insisted on the pose, "in spite of strong objections from Paul Rée."[15] Yet it was Lou who received the photograph from the studio, and when she sent a copy to Rée, he commented that only Nietzsche had come out well and added, "Now you see, Lou, that just for once you were not right."[16] Commentators have studied this picture with close attention, trying to decipher the expressions on the three faces. In a particularly intriguing discussion, David B. Allison suggests that Lou is uncertain and embarrassed, Rée looks confused, and Nietzsche has "a knowing smile."[17] The first two descriptions seem accurate enough to me, but it is hard to see any humor in Nietzsche's self-absorbed stare. This is not necessarily inconsistent with Allison's further interpretation: he suggests that Nietzsche, already motivated by jealous resentment, set up the scene as an elaborate ploy to humiliate Rée by re-enacting an "often retold" medieval story about a trick played on Aristotle at the court of Alexander. That may be the case; yet it should be noted that three years later, an equally staged group photograph was taken of Rée and Lou with the third member of a new "trio," Max Heinemann.[18] In this picture, Lou is again posed in a dominating position over the two men; so one should be cautious in drawing conclusions from the Lucerne photograph.

After this shared journey, Rée returned to Stibbe, where he was soon visited by Lou as a family guest. In August 1882, however, Nietzsche's relationship with Lou was advanced considerably by three weeks spent together in the holiday resort of Tautenburg. Matters were complicated by the presence of the straight-laced Elisabeth Nietzsche, who had come to dislike the younger woman intensely and who disapproved of the three friends' plan to set up a joint household in Paris and attend lectures at the university there. Meanwhile, Lou reported daily to the absent Rée by keeping a diary meant to be read by him, and later made a second visit to Stibbe. The three-way correspondence of this period reveals a good deal of maneuvering by each person, often falling well short of the mutual candor that was their official policy as "free spirits." By November, when they came together again in Leipzig, the concealed tensions had increased, and it became clear that Nietzsche could not remain the third member of the "trinity." Rée and Lou went to stay in Berlin together, parting from Nietzsche at the Leipzig railway station with insincere assurances of a continued shared life. It was the last time that either saw him. A deeply wounded Nietzsche retreated to winter quarters in Rapallo, on the Italian Riviera. In the new year of 1883, his emotional turmoil was accompanied by an intense burst of creativity, and he began a very different kind of literary work by completing the first part of *Thus Spoke Zarathustra* within just ten days.

1880. Later in the same year he traveled to North America, but without enthusiasm for either the people or the scenery. He wrote back, "The long sea voyage (with still or adverse wind almost all the time) has at least strengthened my philosophical muscles, and more a *philosophe* than ever (nothing can be less American!) I am burning to get back to Europe and to work. Even Niagara Falls, which I travel to tomorrow, I regard almost more as a duty than a pleasure."[13]

It was not until the beginning of 1882, a fateful year for both, that the two friends met again. They came together in Genoa, where Nietzsche had established himself to spend the winter for the second time. Nietzsche arranged a nearby lodging for Rée, and they went together to see Sarah Bernhardt performing in "La Dame aux camélias." After a month of renewed intimacy, Rée moved on to Rome, where he rejoined the circle of Malwida von Meysenbug, who had settled there and built up a circle of intellectual friends. In her salon near the Colosseum he met an interesting and unconventional young Russian, Lou Salomé, traveling through Europe with her mother. The two women had brought a letter of introduction to Malwida von Meysenbug, who wrote to Nietzsche telling him about the visitors. "A very remarkable girl (I believe Rée has written to you about her) for whom I, amongst many others, have my book to thank, appears to me to have come to much the same results in philosophical thinking as you, i.e. practical idealism, with a discarding of every metaphysical assumption and concern for the explanation of metaphysical problems. Rée and I agree in the wish to see you together with this extraordinary being, but unfortunately I cannot advise a trip to Rome, since the conditions of life here would not be beneficial to you."[14]

Instead of going to Rome, Nietzsche went on a sea trip to Sicily, only to find the southern wind of Messina an intolerable strain on his nerves. Returning by way of Naples, he joined Rée and Lou in Rome, where they met in the dramatic setting of St. Peter's church. The affinity already established between Rée and Lou quickly became something more complex and unstable: a "trinity" of professed free spirits, intent on creating a new way of living, based solely on shared aspirations and ideals, with neither the constraints of legal ties nor the tensions of sexual relationships. To some extent, the Sorrento period of six years earlier figured as a successful experiment in this direction; however, the new configuration was crucially different in ways that soon became apparent. The relationship between Nietzsche, Rée, and Lou was sabotaged both by external influences—Nietzsche's hostile sister—and by an unacknowledged but intense rivalry between the two men for Lou's loyalty.

Within a few days of the meeting in Rome, all three were traveling north, staying first in Orta in the Italian lake district, and then in Lucerne, where they

Nietzsche found highly amusing.[6] He told Rée that he was taking three books to read on his summer holiday in the Swiss mountain resort of Rosenlauibad: they were "something new from the American Mark Twain" (probably *The Adventures of Tom Sawyer,* recently published in German translation), Plato's *Laws,* and Rée's *The Origin of the Moral Sensations*—a suitable work to read in the vicinity of a glacier, he added.[7] While in Rosenlauibad, Nietzsche made the acquaintance of George Croom Robertson, editor of the English philosophy journal *Mind,* and recommended Rée's book to him.[8] Later that year, an anonymous review—apparently by Croom Robertson himself—appeared in *Mind.*[9] The writer gave a concise summary of the book's argument and commented, "The essay is marked by great lucidity of expression, and no common boldness of thinking. It deserves attention both for the scientific value of some of its observations, and as a rather striking specimen of the pessimistic vein of thought now prominent in Germany."[10] Nietzsche told Rée that Croom Robertson was interested in having the book translated into English, but that did not happen, for the time being.

Rée had hoped to use *The Origin of the Moral Sensations* as a Habilitation thesis to gain a position at one of the German or Swiss universities but, after his cool reception in Jena, decided that a longer and more scholarly elaboration of his theory was more appropriate. Encouraging Nietzsche to publish his own ideas on morality, he presented himself as less a practical moralist than a moral philosopher: "I myself am more of a theorist than ever, and how necessary it is for practical ethics to address the origin of morality theoretically and historically, I see in the study of criminal law. A jurist once said to me that he was astonished how easily philosophers take an assumption for proven. He was right to be astonished. Even the mere distinction between philosophical assumptions and their proofs would in most cases suffice to show the assumptions as unproven or badly proven."[11] Yet Rée's efforts were now directed toward adding a positive historical content to his philosophical theory, drawing upon jurisprudence, history, and anthropology to provide empirical evidence for an account of the development of punishment as a social institution; but the project was not completed until 1885, when it appeared in book form as *Die Entstehung des Gewissens* (*The Origin of Conscience*).

The interests shared by Rée and Nietzsche were not limited to philosophy. Each was preoccupied with his state of health and in correspondence often dwelled at length on physical ailments. "I have had a headache for 14 months without even one minute's respite," Rée claimed in one letter.[12] Not surprisingly, their speculative plans for travel together tended to center upon health resorts of various kinds. Although these ideas went no further, Rée did make a visit of five days with the Nietzsche family in Naumburg at the beginning of

been given a year's leave by his university to recover from recurring ill health. He and his student Albert Brenner, also suffering from health problems, had become friendly with Malwida von Meysenbug, a veteran champion of women's rights, committed Wagnerian, and author of a best-selling autobiography, *Memoiren einer Idealistin* [Memoirs of an idealist]. She invited Brenner and Nietzsche to stay with her in winter accommodation in Sorrento. Nietzsche managed to have the invitation expanded to include Rée, and the three men traveled together to Italy, where they took up quarters at the pensione Villa Rubinacci. For the next five months, Nietzsche and Rée were in daily contact, and they presumably did not always remain silent together, given the considerable overlap between their intellectual interests.[3] Their most important mutual influence would have been through these daily conversations; we can only guess at their themes through the partial evidence of correspondence and later writing. However, the work that each carried out during this period displays many common elements, in both content and style.

During this time Rée became close to Malwida von Meysenbug, who found him a congenial companion, although deploring his philosophical views as lacking in idealism. Rée sometimes reported to Nietzsche's family on the state of Nietzsche's health, touching on other matters as well: for example, writing to Elisabeth Nietzsche, he offered self-deprecating comments on *Psychological Observations*. Elisabeth had apparently said that she had "crossed out" the chapter on women; Rée replied that he would have gone further, and crossed out the whole book as "too one-sided" in its portrayal of human nature.[4] In another letter to Elisabeth, he gallantly praised the female sex for its healthy ignorance of philosophy. "Your sex has no prejudices, no system," he explained, and added that for this reason, women are better psychologists than men, at least in practice. "Anyway," Rée concluded, "when it comes to a second edition of the *Observations,* the chapter 'On Women' must certainly be revised thoroughly. I have gradually arrived at a quite different standpoint. In my next book, you, dear Fräulein, will be a bit more satisfied in this respect; and with the one I intend to write after that, almost completely satisfied."[5]

In April 1877 Rée returned to his family home, and a month later Nietzsche left Sorrento to visit health resorts in Switzerland before resuming his academic duties in Basel (only temporarily, as it turned out). Their friendship continued by correspondence, as Rée made efforts to enter German academic life by gaining his Habilitation in Jena, but he encountered only hostility among the academic philosophers. Back in Stibbe, he was somewhat consoled by the appearance of his book *Der Ursprung der moralischen Empfindungen* (*The Origin of the Moral Sensations*). The copy he sent to Nietzsche carried the inscription "To the father of this work most gratefully from its mother," which

assimilated Jewish families. Ferdinand Rée had become wealthy in business and bought his own country estate at Stibbe, near Tütz (now Tuczno, in Poland), also maintaining a residence in Berlin. Paul Rée attended the Gymnasium in Schwerin and in 1869 became a student of philosophy and law at the University of Leipzig. After a short period of army service during the war between Prussia and France, he attended lectures in Berlin. In 1875 he qualified for his doctorate from Halle with a dissertation on the concept of "the noble" in Aristotle's ethics.

Rée's activities were not, however, directed primarily toward academic scholarship. The monthly allowance he received from his family enabled him to travel about Western Europe, returning from time to time to stay on the Rée estate in West Prussia, and to follow his own interests in reading and writing. He had studied such diverse authors as Darwin and Schopenhauer, and he developed a particular admiration for the French writers La Bruyère, Chamfort, Vauvenargues, and, most of all, La Rochefoucauld, not only as moralists and observers of human nature, but as masters of the aphoristic form of expression. Ambitious to follow their literary and philosophical model, he worked on polishing his own aphorisms with the aim of bringing them together under the general heading of "psychological observations."

Friedrich Nietzsche and Paul Rée had first met in Basel during the summer of 1873, introduced by a common friend, Heinrich Romundt. At that time, Nietzsche was a professor of classical philology, although already moving away from both his discipline and his academic career. Rée attended Nietzsche's lectures on early Greek thought and showed him a manuscript of his aphorisms. When *Psychologische Beobachtungen: Aus dem Nachlass von ✶✶* (*Psychological Observations*) was published anonymously two years later, Nietzsche came across a copy and identified it as Rée's work—apparently by recognizing the observation that being able to remain silent together comfortably is a sign of genuine sympathy. He wrote to Rée, then in Paris, praising his work highly and recommending his publisher Ernst Schmeitzner for any further books: "I say this just because the one thing that I did not like about your book was the last page, where the writings of Eduard von Hartmann are listed; the work of a thinker should never bring to mind the work of a pseudo-thinker."[1] Rée was delighted by this letter and replied in his most ingratiating manner: he regretted not having got to know Nietzsche better in Basel, yet the absence of a personal relationship made Nietzsche's praise all the more welcome. "Only from today onward will I have complete confidence in myself," he wrote.[2]

Rée's short stay in Basel on the way back to Germany at the end of 1875 confirmed the new friendship, and the two men arranged to spend the period between the autumn of 1876 and the following spring together. Nietzsche had

TRANSLATOR'S INTRODUCTION

Paul Rée is a figure remembered today for his friendship with and philosophical influence on another writer: Friedrich Nietzsche. To a lesser extent, he figures in biographies of Lou Andreas-Salomé, again as a personal and intellectual influence during a particular period of her life. Yet Rée is of interest in his own right as a writer and thinker. He was not only a pioneer in the application of the Darwinian theory of natural selection to moral psychology but also an author who tried to continue the tradition of the French moralists in expressing insights into human nature in an aphoristic form. The interest of his work arises largely from the way it combines these two rather different characteristics, and the resulting originality of Rée's approach entitles him to be regarded as a minor but genuine philosopher.

In this volume, Paul Rée's basic contributions to philosophy are presented to an English-speaking audience for the first time. Between them, his first two books include all the main themes in his thinking, as well as displaying the varied styles—aphoristic and essayistic—of his writing. His several later books only revisit the same territory, amplifying earlier treatments while adding little in the way of new ideas or even new expressions. Moreover, for anyone interested in the thought of Nietzsche, it is these two works that are essential reading for the revealing light they throw on Nietzsche's philosophical development. Not only do they confirm the presence of Rée's influence in such works as *Human, All-Too-Human* but they also enable us to see just how Nietzsche moved toward his most original ideas by criticizing and distancing himself from Rée's theories about the origins of conscience and moral judgment. Nietzsche's later thinking remains informed by Rée's concept of a history, or prehistory, of morality—that is, of an inquiry into a crucial development that has been wholly forgotten or suppressed and yet is accessible to the researcher armed with the right intellectual tools. In what follows, we see how this project began.

PAUL RÉE'S LIFE AND WORK

Paul Ludwig Carl Heinrich Rée was born on 21 November 1849 in Bartelshagen, a village in Pomerania, near the Baltic coast. He was the second of three children of Ferdinand and Jenny Rée (née Jonas), who were both from

ACKNOWLEDGMENTS

This work was made possible by an outside studies program granted by Monash University during the second half of 1997. I was a visiting scholar in the School of Education and Professional Development at the University of East Anglia during that period, and I wish to express my gratitude to colleagues there, and in particular David Bridges, for their hospitality and support. Access to primary sources and background materials was provided by the British Library and the Cambridge University Library. In the latter case, I am especially grateful to Lynne Broughton for her assistance during my time in Cambridge.

More recently, I have benefited from the friendly help and advice of Tracy Strong in bringing this project to completion. In the later stages of preparation, Mary Small gave valuable assistance in checking the translations for accuracy and sensitivity to German usage and in suggesting many improvements.

This volume is dedicated to the memory of my friend Reg Hollingdale.

—Robin Small

CONTENTS

Basic Writings combines English translations of
Psychologische Beobachtungen (1875) and *Der Ursprung der
moralischen Empfindungen* (1877).

Library of Congress Cataloging-in-Publication Data
Rée, Paul, 1849–1901.
[Ursprung der moralischen Empfindungen. English]
Basic writings / Paul Rée ; translated from the German
and edited by Robin Small.
p. cm. — (International Nietzsche studies)
Includes bibliographical references.
ISBN 978-0-252-02818-2 (cloth : alk. paper)
1. Philosophy. I. Rée, Paul, 1849–1901. Psychologische
Beobachtungen aus dem Empfindungen. English.
II. Small, Robin, 1944– . III. Title. IV. Series.
B3323.R343U67   2003
193—dc21   2002013303

BASIC WRITINGS

PAUL RÉE

Translated from the German and
Edited by

Robin Small

University of Illinois Press
Urbana, Chicago, and Springfield

BASIC WRITINGS

INTERNATIONAL NIETZSCHE STUDIES

Nietzsche has emerged as a thinker of extraordinary importance, not only in the history of philosophy but in many fields of contemporary inquiry. Nietzsche studies are maturing and flourishing in many parts of the world. This internationalization of inquiry with respect to Nietzsche's thought and significance may be expected to continue.

International Nietzsche Studies is conceived as a series of monographs and essay collections that will reflect and contribute to these developments. The series will present studies in which responsible scholarship is joined to the analysis, interpretation, and assessment of the many aspects of Nietzsche's thought that bear significantly upon matters of moment today. In many respects Nietzsche is our contemporary, with whom we do well to reckon, even when we find ourselves at odds with him. The series is intended to promote this reckoning, embracing diverse interpretive perspectives, philosophical orientations, and critical assessments.

The series is also intended to contribute to the ongoing reconsideration of the character, agenda, and prospects of philosophy itself. Nietzsche was much concerned with philosophy's past, present, and future. He sought to affect not only its understanding but also its practice. The future of philosophy is an open question today, thanks at least in part to Nietzsche's challenge to the philosophical traditions of which he was so critical. It remains to be seen—and determined—whether philosophy's future will turn out to resemble the "philosophy of the future" to which he proffered a prelude and of which he provided a preview, by both precept and practice. But this is a possibility we do well to take seriously. International Nietzsche Studies will attempt to do so, while contributing to the understanding of Nietzsche's philosophical thinking and its bearing upon contemporary inquiry.

—Richard Schacht

lished two years later.[32] Instead, he follows Schopenhauer in asserting that human happiness is a rare and fleeting phenomenon and that any notion that moral virtue increases one's chances of achieving happiness is contradicted by an observation of human affairs. It is not morality, Rée concludes, as much as rationality and self-control that offers our best available guidelines in the conduct of life.

EVOLUTIONARY ETHICS AND THE PROBLEM OF ALTRUISM

Rée's theoretical relation to Darwin is worth exploring in more detail, in view of his importance as a pioneer in the application of the theory of evolution to moral experience. The difficulties faced by evolutionary ethics in gaining credibility in philosophy were due, in part, to a widespread preoccupation with the "naturalistic fallacy" supposedly involved in any linking of moral concepts with scientific facts about human origins. Yet there were also issues for the theory of natural selection that were not addressed until a century had passed since *The Origin of Species*. As Daniel Dennett has pointed out, Rée and Spencer imagined that they could see "a straight, simple path to altruism" by way of group selection.[33] In the long run, this straightforward approach to an explanation of altruism turned out to face insoluble problems. Important later debates not only brought these out but gave rise to different interpretations of natural selection, and we need to be aware of these when placing Rée's approach in historical perspective.

As we have seen, Rée's inquiry is premised on the reality of the non-egoistic feelings and actions that, like Schopenhauer, he takes to constitute the basis of morality. He rejects the claim made by writers such as Helvétius that some selfish motive will be discovered for even the most morally praiseworthy behavior. Although the prevalence of egoism is far greater than we commonly imagine, there remain intractable cases of selflessness that need to be explained along different lines. Assuming that there is such a thing as altruism, then, how can it be explained? As with vanity, Rée has two answers, one referring to individual development and the other to the evolution of the species. The first explanation relies on the concept of habituation: we are trained from childhood to behave in ways that benefit others and to avoid actions that harm others, so that these patterns of behavior become second nature, although their motives remain weaker in general than our selfish drives. The other answer, that unselfish drives are innate, is taken directly from Darwin himself: "social" instincts occur naturally in the human species, having arisen as variations that were then favored by natural selection, since groups that practice mutual support and cooperation have an advantage in the struggle for existence. As with vanity, there is some overlap between these explanations, owing to the principle of heritability of acquired characteristics, which was accepted by Darwin as having some validity, although it came to be repudiated by most of his later followers as an unsupported and superfluous postulate.

The main point of reference for much of *The Origin of the Moral Sensations* is Darwin's treatment of morality in the second part of *The Descent of Man,* which was published in 1870–71. The context is a discussion of the mental differences between human beings and other animals. Darwin asserts that all such differences are of degree and not of kind, and he denies that any quality is "absolutely peculiar to man."[34] Accordingly, he is skeptical about the distinction between instincts and intelligence. Animals show emotion, memory, imagination "and even some power of reasoning."[35] Further, even abstract thinking and language, so often named as distinctively human, have some counterpart in the animals. Just as newborns lack all the mental powers of an adult and yet gradually develop those powers, so too the course of evolution has enabled species to do the same thing.

Turning from these mental abilities to moral feeling and judgment, Darwin begins by allowing that the most important single difference between human beings and the "lower" animals is the moral sense, or conscience, but he notes that this has never been approached from the side of natural history. Human beings are social animals whose ancestors probably lived in extended families bound together by instinctive love and sympathy.[36] Many species are social and unite for protection and mutual care, as well as cooperating in hunting and food gathering. Whether they feel sympathy is hard to say, Darwin concedes: often they are insensitive to one another, but then, so are people. Certainly animals often do sympathize with others' distress or danger, and dogs and elephants show a sense of loyalty to their human masters. The social behavior of animals points to strong instincts operating apart from pleasure and pain. First and foremost, there are the parental and filial affections, and it is from these, Darwin suggests, that broader social sympathies probably developed, with the assistance of natural selection.

In this way, Darwin traces the moral sense back to the social instincts of species that live together in families and more extended groupings. However, it is important to note the limitation of these patterns of behavior. Anthropologists have observed that primitive peoples practice moral behavior only within their own tribe. Hence, Darwin writes, "actions are regarded by savages, and were probably so regarded by primeval man, as good or bad, solely as they obviously affect the welfare of the tribe—not that of the species, nor that of an individual member of the tribe."[37] Of course, this restricted application constitutes a low degree of morality by our familiar standards. But the qualities developed in a narrow context come to be extended more broadly as a greater understanding is acquired, and so it is that the moral character of humanity gradually improves.

Darwin is aware that an account of human morality as having evolved from the instincts found in other species is likely to be controversial. He considers the objection that morality cannot be reduced to instinct: how can an impulsive action, carried out without deliberation, be called moral? Darwin replies that there is no clear distinction here. Surely our habitual behavior does not cease to be moral simply because deliberation is not present on each occasion? On the contrary, we expect moral virtues to be immediately effective in producing actions. Action out of instinct or habit is quite common in human beings, as in animals, and the assumption that every act has a distinct motive, associated with some pleasure or pain, is simply false.[38] Moreover, it is impossible to draw any clear line of distinction between impulsive and deliberate actions. Many highly admirable actions, such as saving another person's life in an emergency, are done quite spontaneously. It would be absurd, Darwin concludes, to regard them as less moral than thoughtful choices or decisions that come out of a struggle between opposing motives.

What, then, is the criterion for morality? If we cannot specify it in terms of moral *motives,* as this argument seems to show, we can at least refer moral actions to a type of *agent.* Darwin explains: "A moral being is one who is capable of comparing his past and future actions or motives, and of approving or disapproving of them."[39] The human mental faculties are very active in reminding us of others, their judgments, and welfare. Further, language enables public opinion to become a strong influence. Our other instincts are far less present in our minds, except on temporary occasions. Hence arises the phenomenon of conscience: if another impulse prevails, we will feel remorse or shame. But long habit promotes a self-command that prevents such lapses; and Darwin speculates (as he had done in *The Origin of Species*) that characteristics acquired in this way may be passed down to later generations.[40] He sums up: "Ultimately our moral sense or conscience becomes a highly complex sentiment—originating in the social instincts, largely guided by the approbation of our fellow-men, ruled by reason, self-interest, and in later times by deep religious feelings, and confirmed by instruction and habit."[41]

In his discussion of morality, Darwin maintains a cautious distance from the utilitarianism of his contemporaries. He suggests that social instincts should be seen as aiming at the general good or welfare of the community, rather than at its general happiness. As sympathy becomes more sensitive, we do take the happiness of others as our standard. But the primary impulse behind moral action is still the social instinct—which, Darwin notes, leads to our regarding the approbation and disapprobation of others—and this is guided, but not replaced, by some rational principle such as the greatest happiness of the greatest number. He does, however, endorse Spencer's suggestion that past experiences of utility have given rise to inherited tendencies to moral feelings that are no longer directly linked with utility—a thesis crucial to Rée's argument as well.[42]

The main problem concerning the moral sense, for Darwin, concerns regret or remorse. Why do we feel that we ought to obey one natural instinct rather than another? And why do we experience regret after obeying some impulse other than the social instinct? Animals seem, on the face of it, to have no such feelings. Yet in animals, the social instinct may well come into conflict with other instincts. Darwin argues that any animal with social instincts will acquire a moral sense as its intellectual powers develop. For it will find pleasure in assisting others of its species, within limits, and tend to remember past actions and motives more strongly then ephemeral desires such as hunger. Of course, other animals, if they came to have equally active mental powers, would have a moral sense different in *content* from ours—but still, they would have a moral sense if their social instinct acquired a similar permanence and similar links with the approval and disapproval of others. "Any instinct, permanently stronger or more enduring than another, gives rise to a feeling which we express by saying that it ought to be obeyed. A pointer dog, if able to reflect on his past conduct, would say to himself, I ought (as indeed we say of him) to have pointed at that hare and not yielded to the passing temptation of hunting it."[43] Elsewhere Darwin discusses the analogous case of the swallow who deserts her young, overcome by the temporary but very strong instinct to migrate. Normally, the maternal instinct is supreme, but at this time the other is more powerful and prevails. Darwin comments, "When arrived at the end of her long journey, and the migratory instinct has ceased to act, what an agony of remorse the bird would feel, if, from being endowed with great mental activity, she could not prevent the image constantly passing through her mind, of her young ones perishing in the bleak north from cold and hunger."[44] Similarly with human beings, he argues, remorse is felt when a passing impulse has led to behavior in conflict with the far more enduring social instinct.

While Rée follows Darwin's account in general, he disagrees on this point. Darwin suggests that the pain of conscience is the frustration of a natural instinct to care for others, and he emphasizes the similarity with other instincts. He writes, "After having yielded to some temptation we feel a sense of dissatisfaction, shame, repentance, or remorse, analogous to the feelings caused by other powerful instincts or desires, when left unsatisfied or baulked."[45] Rée objects that the frustration of the instinct of sympathy cannot be identified with a bad conscience any more than the frustration of some egoistic drive such as revenge. Hence, he rejects Darwin's claim that a bird deserting its young to migrate would experience a guilty conscience, if it had the mental capacity to reflect on its behavior. We find it natural to imagine this, but in doing so we are only imagining how we would feel in that situation, given our upbringing and training. Rée argues that there is just a conflict of instincts here, and a bird staying behind would experience just as much frustration.[46] Darwin, he insinuates, was misled by his own moral bias toward family loyalty into giving this class of instincts a privileged status in relation to others.

Is Rée's objection a reasonable one? His argument seems to be that if moral regret were just a sense of frustration, we would experience such a feeling on failing to satisfy *any* instinct, even a very egoistic one. In fact, Darwin is simplifying his own theory when he gives hypothetical examples in which a social instinct is enhanced only by a modest capacity for memory or "reflection," and then uses an expression like "remorse" to describe the outcome. On the account he gives elsewhere, a number of factors are required for the formation of a moral sense: the unusual stability and constancy of the social instinct, its reinforcement by a desire for the approval of others, the communication of their expectations through language, a more or less extended process of upbringing and habituation, not only memory but also foresight, and so on. With so much social mediation involved, moral feelings can hardly be simply identified with the frustration of some instinct. At the same time, Darwin is concerned to emphasize the continuity between human beings and other species. His fanciful images of remorse-stricken birds or dogs are designed to convey this continuity, rather than to assert a close similarity. In other words, he is simplifying in these examples for a particular purpose of illustration and persuasion.

One could also question whether Rée is doing himself justice here. He denies that the pain of conscience can consist in the frustration of some instinct. Yet what else could it be based upon, according to a naturalistic theory? Rée's tendency to intellectualize, which Nietzsche would later identify as the weakness of his moral theory, is seen in the close attention he gives to moral discourse, which he interprets as based on misconceptions (such as the belief in free will) and systematically misleading usages (such as the abbreviation of "good for . . ." as simply "good"). The original sources of the moral sensations tend to be hidden under the elaborate presentation of this superstructure. Thus the appearance arises of a conflict between Rée's emphasis on the specificity of the moral sense and Darwin's emphasis on the continuity between human beings and other species, in mental as well as physical respects.

The main problem area in Darwin's account of morality, as well as Rée's, concerns the operation of natural selection. There is not much mention of natural selection in Darwin's chapter on conscience, but later in *The Descent of Man* he argues for progress in morality based on the selection of groups that have gained an advantage in the struggle for existence by virtue of their moral behavior:

> It must not be forgotten that although a high standard of morality gives but a slight or no advantage to each individual man and his children over the other men of the same tribe, yet that an increase in the number of well-endowed men and advancement in the standard of morality will certainly give an immense advantage to one tribe over another. There can be no doubt that a tribe including many members who, from possessing in a high degree the spirit of patriotism, fidelity, obedience, courage, and sympathy, were always ready to aid one another, and to sacrifice themselves for the common good, would be victorious over most other tribes; and this would be natural selection. At all times throughout the world tribes have supplanted other tribes; and as morality is one important element in their success, the standard of morality and the number of well-endowed men will thus everywhere tend to rise and increase.[47]

What makes this an untypical argument for Darwin is the idea of group rather than individual selection. His usual claim is that some quality is selected because it gives the individual organism an advantage in the struggle for existence. The qualities he mentions here do not give an individual an advantage over other individuals—in fact, they seem likely to be a severe disadvantage. Yet a group whose members have these qualities has an advantage over other groups—assuming that support and loyalty are limited to other members of the group, and are accompanied by a strong hostility toward all outsiders. This last point suggests a grim picture of humanity as whole. However, Darwin should not be accused of any celebration of a war of all against all, either among individuals or among groups; for he also notes that habit and education do more than natural selection to improve moral qualities.[48]

Group selection is a debated concept, and even its defenders are concerned to define the conditions under which it might be a plausible explanation. The theoretical problem is this: if altruism is a disadvantage for the individual, how could it appear in groups in the first place? Random variation is the standard answer, as for other traits, mental as well as physical. The real issue concerns the likelihood that this variation would persist or even increase in frequency. After all, as Darwin points out, "the struggle almost invariably will be most severe between the individuals of the same species, for they frequent the same districts, require the same food, and are exposed to the same dangers."[49] Even if groups practicing mutual altruism were to arise in some chance fashion, would they not be undermined by the presence of egoistic individuals who have an advantage over other members and therefore must eventually come to predominate in the group?

One answer is that the disadvantages experienced by unselfish individuals within a mixed group may be outweighed by the advantages of that group in its competition with groups that contain more (or only) selfish individuals. In that case, the number of altruists in the species as a whole will tend to increase after all, since the successful group will have more descendants.[50] Rée touches on a similar line of thought in *The Origin of the Moral Sensations.* He freely acknowledges the disadvantages of altruism for the individual: "It is self-evident that non-egoistic individuals have no prospect of leaving behind more descendants than egoistic individuals." On the other hand, groups derive great benefit from this quality: "When the members of a tribe of *animals* have a relatively strong social instinct, the stronger cohesion, caring and fighting for one another that this provides gives this tribe an immense superiority in conflict with other tribes." Although Rée does not spell it out, his assumption must be that this factor is a much stronger influence than the first one, and that its primacy explains the original growth in unselfish behavior. But how far do these considerations apply to human beings in their state of civilization? Here Rée takes a pessimistic view. Patriotism, he suggests, has become all but unnecessary in modern society, since selfish motives (such as ambition or the sense of honor) are used to serve the same end of promoting the common safety and welfare. Hence, he concludes, the pressure of natural selection to encourage "moral progress," in the sense of a growth in non-egoistic feeling and behavior, is no longer in operation. At best, we can look forward to a further "domestication" of human nature through closer social control.

This argument admits group selection as a explanatory principle alongside individual selection—yet only under certain circumstances. For one thing, it presupposes strong rivalry between different groups. A universal peace would allow selfishness to reassert itself within each of these groups, with disastrous consequences, unless held in check by the kinds of substitutes for altruism that Rée describes. The argument also implies a strict limitation of altruism to members of one's own tribe: in fact, unthinking hostility toward outsiders will be favored by the same process of group selection. But the main problem here concerns the relative importance of group and individual selection. Darwin writes of the latter: "It may be said that natural selection is daily and hourly scrutinising, throughout the world, every variation, even the slightest; rejecting that which is bad, preserving and adding up all that is good, silently and insensibly working, whenever and wherever opportunity offers, at the improvement of each organic being in relation to its organic and inorganic conditions of life."[51] This process acts on every aspect of every organism, making no distinction between inner and outer or between physical and behavioral characteristics. It is hard to see how any tendency at a group level can match the power of such a pervasive influence, one which, Darwin goes on to observe, "can act only through and for the good of each being." In consequence, the power of group selection to account for the phenomenon of altruism is still open to serious doubt.

Given these difficulties, later evolutionary theorists have modified the concept of altruism by calling upon two further concepts, which I will refer to as *reciprocity* and *nepotism*. The first of these assumes that helping others gives the individual an advantage in circumstances where a return can be expected from them. The second idea is a generalization of the parental and family loyalties that are known to be present in many species. The question then is whether, as Robert L. Trivers puts it, "models that attempt to explain altruistic behavior in terms of natural selection are models designed to take the altruism out of altruism."[52] Let us look briefly at each of these theoretical options in turn.

Reciprocity may be either direct, where benefit is expected from the recipient, or indirect, where the return is expected from others. By contributing to a general goodwill, the individual's chances of receiving benefits may outweigh the cost of selfless acts. Helping others without immediate reward can thus be to one's advantage, given a set of established expectations within a social group that has agreed to share interests. It is important to note that the explanation in terms of possible reciprocity does not imply that altruistic behavior is "really" selfish, in the sense of being motivated by a desire to gain these later benefits. After all, sexual behavior is not usually motivated by a wish to reproduce, although its existence is presumably to be explained in terms of its reproductive function. A psychological explanation of behavior in terms of some drive is one thing, but an evolutionary explanation of that drive in terms of natural selection is another. The theory of reciprocal altruism has been reinforced by games theory, which enables an assessment of the outcomes of strategies followed by "players" over a period of time. This model confirms that a policy of altruism, subject to suspension upon a lack of reciprocity in others, can produce a stable social situation, and even one which produces greater benefits for the participants than other strategies. Further, the theory also takes in various psychological aspects of morality and explains the selection of certain patterns of motivation—both moral and immoral.[53]

Nepotism is a concept that begins with an understanding of fitness as reproductive success. Parental care for offspring clearly contributes to such fitness, although it is often unlikely to benefit the parent, either directly or indirectly through future reciprocity. But individuals do not literally reproduce themselves: rather, they pass on some of their genes. The concept of "inclusive fitness" does not regard the individual organism as the subject of natural selection but rather the gene (a concept unavailable to Darwin). This enables the theory to explain the many instances of sacrifice made by parents for their offspring: such acts ensure that their genes will be passed on. To a lesser extent, it accounts for altruism directed toward other related individuals, that is, toward those who share at least some of the same genes, and so are as able to pass those on as the altruistic individual. Hence, sacrificing one's life to save siblings may be a token of "inclusive fitness."[54] There is no reciprocity here, because the interests of the individual are not the point. In one sense, this account does "take the altruism out of altruism" in that it reduces the altruism of the individual person to the (metaphorical) selfishness of the gene that is selected through individual self-sacrifice. But if the task is to account for the puzzling phenomenon of non-egoistic behavior, kin selection does provide an explanation, at least within the limits of close genetic relationships.

It is noticeable that Rée's evolutionary explanation for vanity does not face these problems, because it works at the level of individual selection. Observations of the prevalence of vanity in human nature provide strong supporting evidence: this is just what one would expect to find when a quality has been favored by natural selection over many generations. But altruism is another matter, and neither of these later extensions of the theory of evolution offers much support for Rée's theory as it is presented in *The Origin of the Moral Sensations*. His concept of morality is still that of Schopenhauer, in which moral goodness is identified with a selfless benevolence that is unconditional and indiscriminate—that is, which has nothing to do with past or future reciprocity and is directed toward strangers as much as toward offspring, other family members, or even other members of the same tribe. The "straight, simple path to altruism" entailed in Rée's reliance on group selection, as observed by Dennett, corresponds to this immediate universality: what needs to be explained is taken to be a simple quality of feeling and action. Later versions of evolutionary ethics have been less constrained by commitment to a particular conception of morality and more open to finding explanatory mechanisms for the motives involved in moral life, even if that does mean, in some sense, qualifying the concept of altruism. In Rée's defense, one could note that contemporary writers such as Spencer were also biased by their philosophical convictions in attempting an evolutionary approach to morality. The person who most consistently avoided such temptations in applying the Darwinian theory of evolution to the "moral sense" was, as we noted earlier, Charles Darwin.

NIETZSCHE'S PATH FROM RÉEALISM TO ANTI-RÉEALISM

Paul Rée's relation to Friedrich Nietzsche has often been discussed by commentators. One common view is that Rée exerted a temporary but beneficial influence by separating Nietzsche from Schopenhauerian metaphysics and introducing him to scientific rationalism, as well as inspiring a plainer and more disciplined mode of expression. This is certainly more accurate than the summary judgment of Karl Jaspers that "Nietzsche learned hardly anything from Rée."[55] The full story is more subtle, especially in its later phase, and it goes deeper into Nietzsche's philosophical development toward a radical "revaluation of all values," a process in which his thinking first with, and then against, Paul Rée was a crucial factor.

The earliest and plainest evidence of Rée's influence is found in Nietzsche's book *Human, All-Too-Human*, which the author sent to his friend with a message: "It *belongs* to you—to others it is only given."[56] The work contains a number of direct references to Rée, especially in the first division, entitled "On the History of the Moral Sensations." Under the heading "Advantages of Psychological Observation," Nietzsche complains that the tradition of La Rochefoucauld and "those related to him in style and spirit" is not acknowledged in today's society as a source of insight into human nature.[57] In the next section, his point of reference is made explicit: "La Rochefoucauld and those other French masters of soul-searching (to whom there has recently been added a German, the author of *Psychological Observations*) are like skilful marksmen who again and again hit the black circle—but it is the black of human nature."[58] Such psychological observation, Nietzsche argues, is even more valuable to science than it is to the individual person, because it supplies a body of empirical material that is not biased by metaphysical or religious interpretation. "For what is the principle which one of the boldest and coldest of thinkers, the author of the book *On* [sic] *The Origin of the Moral Sensations*, arrived at by virtue of his incisive and penetrating analyses of human action? 'Moral man,' he says, 'stands no closer to the intelligible (metaphysical) world than physical man.'"[59] This proposition, Nietzsche comments, once "hardened and sharpened" under the hammer of historical knowledge, will prove a devastating weapon against the supposed "metaphysical need" of the human mind.[60]

Elsewhere in *Human, All-Too-Human*, themes of *The Origin of the Moral Sensations* such as the illusion of free will and the prevalence of human vanity are covered in ways very close to Rée's treatment.[61] Like Rée, Nietzsche argues from causal determinism to the irrationality of punishment as usually understood, asserting that the guilt for a crime, if such a thing exists at all, should be located in educators, parents and society, not in the criminal.[62]

Sometimes Nietzsche's aphorisms are strongly reminiscent of Rée's *Psychological Observations*. To take a single example: under the heading "Preference for particular virtues," Nietzsche writes, "We do not place special importance on possessing a virtue until we perceive its complete absence in our opponent."[63] The thought expressed here is close to Rée's aphorism "Every wife prizes most highly the qualities in men that are lacking in her husband."[64] Only the setting has been slightly (and rather amusingly) altered.

In the further volume published two years later under the title *The Wanderer and His Shadow*, Nietzsche gives a concise paraphrase of Rée's central argument about the hidden origin of moral ideas, presenting it as his own line of thought.

> The same actions that within primitive society were first performed with a view to common *utility* have later been performed by other generations from other motives: out of fear or reverence for those who demanded and recommended them, or out of habit, because one had seen them done all around one from childhood on, or out of benevolence, because their performance generally produced joy and approving faces, or out of vanity, because they were commended. Such actions, whose basic motive, that of utility, has been *forgotten*, are then called *moral* actions: not because, for instance, they are performed out of those *other* motives, but because they are *not* performed from any conscious reason of utility.[65]

Yet different themes also appear alongside these echoes. One is important for Nietzsche's own later thinking: the difference in moral thinking between the strong and weak members of societies. For the ruling tribes and castes, the power to repay benefit with benefit, and harm with harm, is what is called good. Hence, the enemy is not called evil, as one can see in Homer, for whom the Trojan and Greek are both good. On the other hand, the powerless are fearful of others, and so think of everyone else—even the gods—as evil. Nietzsche concludes that since no society could survive a prevalence of that attitude, it is clear that our present values must have come from those of ruling groups.[66] None of this is found in Rée's work of that time: the theme of power is Nietzsche's own, and was to become central to his later thought.

One feature of *Human, All-Too-Human* that can readily be linked with Rée is a dramatic change in Nietzsche's style of expression, a move away from the often blustering manner of *The Birth of Tragedy* and *Untimely Meditations* toward a prose that is spare, disciplined, and free of conventional mannerisms. In his notebooks, Nietzsche gave himself instructions: to avoid long sentences or, where they prove unavoidable, to make their logical structure evident. "Clarity is the first demand," he wrote.[67] Even so, his "cool" manner cannot be mistaken for Rée's relatively abstract and often repetitive mode of exposition. It is governed by a stronger grasp of rhetorical form, and accompanied by a more deliberate consideration of the relation between writer and read-er.[68] There is greater variation of style and tempo in *Human, All-Too-Human* than in Rée's writing, and this flexibility becomes even more noticeable in Nietzsche's later work, where aphoristic formulations are skillfully integrated within longer structures. Even where Nietzsche does seem to accept the discipline of scientific discourse, it is often a calculated strategy on his part rather than any firm commitment to Rée's model.

Clearly, however, Nietzsche was inspired by the aphoristic style. The chapter titles of *Human, All-Too-Human* (and of later works such as *Beyond Good and Evil*) follow those of *Psychological Observations* closely, as do some of the aphorisms themselves. However, Nietzsche's talent for the aphorism was already as great as Rée's, and was soon to become greater. Or rather, he came to use the aphoristic style for a more ambitious purpose: not to make an isolated observation but to condense a greater content. In his own words, "An aphorism, properly stamped and moulded, has not yet been 'deciphered' when it has simply been read off; rather, now its *interpretation* has to begin, for which an art of interpretation is required."[69] Nietzsche's aphorisms lend themselves to expansion and commentary in a way that Rée's generally do not, despite the claim he makes at the beginning of *Psychological Observations* for their status as a "thought concentrate." Rée himself acknowledged something of the kind when he described Nietzsche's "Every word is a prejudice"[70] as "the best aphorism ever made" and added, "It contains a whole philosophy."[71]

With the publication of *Human, All-Too-Human* at hand, Nietzsche found himself in several minds about his change of direction and was reluctant to treat his earlier works as superseded by the new outlook. This led him into a strange attempt to bring out the book under the pseudonym Bernhard Cron. He approached his publisher Ernst Schmeitzner, who had just issued Rée's *The Origin of the Moral Sensations,* with a request that included a fictitious description of the supposed author: "Herr Bernhard Cron is, so far as is known, a German from the Russian Baltic provinces, who of late years has been a continual traveler. In Italy, where among other things he devoted himself to philological and antiquarian studies, he made the acquaintance of Dr Paul Rée. Through the latter's agency he came into contact with Herr Schmeitzner. As his address for the next few years is subject to constant changes, letters should be forwarded to Herr Cron's publisher. Herr Schmeitzner has never seen him personally."[72] No doubt Nietzsche was looking forward to engaging in correspondence as "Bernhard Cron"; but this was not to be. Schmeitzner would have none of the idea. He wrote back to Nietzsche, accompanying the first proof sheets with a peremptory refusal: "One thing I must expressly request, that is, the book should not appear under a pseudonym."[73] To present it as the first output of a new author would be, Schmeitzner added, "the greatest risk" for a publisher, especially given the volume's relatively high price. Nietzsche replied with a certain embarrassment, accepting the decision as coming from someone who is "naturally a better judge than I can be."[74]

Bernhard Cron is, of course, quite similar to Paul Rée. It is hard to believe that Nietzsche did not have in mind the anonymity of Rée's *Psychological Observations* as his model here. However, there was more to the proposal. A revealing document is the draft of a letter to Richard and Cosima Wagner, in which Nietzsche defended the idea of publication under a pseudonym, and gave three separate reasons.[75] He did not want to interfere with the influence of his earlier works, he explained. Moreover, he was trying to keep his name out of further public controversy, for the sake of his health and peace of mind. Finally, he wanted to encourage "an objective discussion" of the book among his friends, without making them feel obliged to refrain from criticism. He added: "But I know none of them who would have the opinions of *this* book, although I am very curious about the objections that will be offered in this case." The first statement is a plain falsehood, since Nietzsche was well aware that his friend Paul Rée shared the general outlook of *Human, All-Too-Human*, but he did not want the Wagners to be aware of that awkward fact. They had met Rée when he and Nietzsche were at the 1876 Bayreuth festival, as well as during the following Sorrento period, and taken an instant dislike to him. This may have been simply due to their fervent anti-Semitism, but there were other reasons, such as Rée's open sympathy with French culture, a perennial object of Wagner's hostility after his earlier experiences in Paris. Even Rée's admiration for Schopenhauer was unacceptable from the Wagnerian point of view, since it explicitly set aside his doctrine of spiritual redemption in favor of a mere worldly wisdom.

Nietzsche was playing a double game, trying to keep his options open as long as possible. He wanted to postpone a break with Bayreuth, already made suspicious by the ambiguities of the fourth *Untimely Meditation*, "Richard Wagner in Bayreuth." Yet such a pretence could be kept up only until the Wagners saw the new book. Its dedication to Voltaire ("the greatest liberator of the spirit") was an offence in itself: as Cosima Wagner remarked, with some justice, Voltaire would never have understood *The Birth of Tragedy*.[76] Nor were the couple deceived by Nietzsche's elimination of explicit references to Richard Wagner and his use in their place of coded expressions such as "the artist," in sections clearly expressing a loss of confidence in the Wagnerian program.[77] They were appalled, and Cosima had no doubt what was to blame for Nietzsche's change of heart. It was the influence of "Israel"—"in the form of a Dr Rée, very sleek, very cool, at the same time as being wrapped up in Nietzsche and dominated by him, though actually outwitting him."[78] Wagner commented bitterly that the book explained Nietzsche's increasing absences from their circle: "I can understand why Rée's company is more congenial to him than mine."[79] It quickly became evident to Nietzsche that he had been, as he put it, "excommunicated" from Bayreuth.[80]

Wagner took a more direct revenge with a signed article in the *Bayreuther Blätter* which, without naming Nietzsche, attacked the new "historical school" in German philosophy for its uncritical and dogmatic use of natural science and, in particular, of chemistry and physics. He complained that the scientific approach, with its hostility toward everything metaphysical, could not account for intuitive knowledge, attempting instead to explain artistic genius in terms of naturally occurring human traits, such as willfulness or a one-sided personal development—a pointed choice of examples, given some of the personal observations in Nietzsche's ostensibly admiring essay on Wagner. The article concluded in a slightly different vein with some pious reflections on the Gospels, including one further allusion to Nietzsche: "Who knows Jesus? Historical criticism, perchance? It casts in its lot with Judaism [*Judentum*], and, just like any Jew, it wonders that the bells on Sunday morn should be ringing for a Jew once crucified two thousand years ago."[81]

Warned in advance of the article by Ernst Schmeitzner, Nietzsche commented, "That W. is objecting to me *publicly* is just what I want, I hate all hiding and hearsay in opposition."[82] Despite this pose of defiance, however, his anxiety about Rée's presence in *Human, All-Too-Human* was made worse by the reactions of other readers who were familiar with his earlier work and, in some cases, had given it public support. When his friend Erwin Rohde accused him of "suddenly becoming Rée," he responded sharply: "By the way, look for only *me* in my book and not my friend Rée. I am proud to have discovered his fine qualities and goals, but he has had *not the slightest* influence on the conception of my 'philosophia in nuce': it was *ready* and in large part committed to paper when I made his closer acquaintance in autumn 1876."[83] Soon after, Nietzsche was writing to Rée in a different tone: "*All* my friends are now agreed that my book comes from and is written *by you*: so I congratulate you on this new authorship (in case your good opinion has not changed) . . . Long live Réealism and my good friend!"[84]

The assimilation of Nietzsche's ideas to Rée's took a new form when their common publisher Ernst Schmeitzner (recommended to Rée by Nietzsche) advertised their books together inside his 1880 bestseller, Eugen Dühring's *Robert Mayer der Galilei des neunzehnten Jahrhunderts* [Robert Mayer, the Galileo of the nineteenth century], and presented Nietzsche as a follower of Rée's philosophical program. "As a moralist, Nietzsche arrives by way of the historical approach at very fruitful conclusions; e.g. the grounding of morality in metaphysics, as proposed by Schopenhauer, is found to be untenable, since historical philosophy has already achieved a natural history of the development of morality: in the work of Paul Rée listed below, *Der Ursprung der moralischen Empfindungen,* which is broadened and developed by Nietzsche."[85] That sort of supporting role was not Nietzsche's conception of his work, though, and his later attempts to dissociate himself from Rée should be seen against the background of this unwelcome interpretation, or misinterpretation, of their relationship. Apart from the breakdown in their personal relations, he was motivated to distance himself from "Réealism" in order to vindicate the independence of his thinking in its changing direction.

This distancing is visible in *Daybreak,* published in 1881. There are two ways of denying morality, Nietzsche explains there. One is to claim that the moral motives that people claim to lie behind their actions are not the real ones; in other words, that people commonly deceive others and themselves as well. The other way of denying morality is to claim that moral judgments are not even true. Nietzsche comments, "This is *my* point of view: though I should be the last to deny that *in very many cases* there is some ground for the other point of view—that is, the point of view of La Rochefoucauld and others who think like him—may also be justified and in any event of great application."[86] The last reference is no doubt to Paul Rée, like the similar one in *Human, All-too-Human.* In contrast with Nietzsche, Rée was never willing to place in question the *value* of morality, understood in his case as the standard which commends altruism and condemns selfishness. In section 5 of *Psychological Observations,* he denies that philosophy undertakes any revaluation of moral values, or even provides any support for them, since we are already certain of their validity. "That a person's goodness lies in the degree of his disinterested concern for the fate of others, and his practical rationality in not following momentary inclinations but taking the future into account, and that people ought to be good and rational, everyone knows by himself and does not need to learn from moral philosophy." Philosophy is not for moral improvement, Rée concludes, any more than art. If metaphysics were, as Kant supposed, an insight into a higher realm from which moral values come, it would presumably make us better people. As it is, philosophy can only contribute to our knowledge and understanding, in the same way as natural science.

After the personal break, Rée continued to speak highly of Nietzsche, according to one source.[87] However, Nietzsche's references to Rée were all dismissive. In 1883 he told several friends that Rée had wanted to dedicate his next book to him, and that he had turned down the offer.[88] When *The Origin of Conscience* finally appeared in 1885, Nietzsche described it in scathing terms: "Yesterday I saw Rée's book on conscience: how empty, how boring, how false! One should write only about things of which one has one's own experience." Yet later in the same letter, Nietzsche has second thoughts and returns to the subject to qualify his judgment, or at least to make a distinction. "I forgot to say how highly I can appreciate the simple, clear and almost antique form of Rée's book. This is the 'philosophical habitus.'—A pity there is not more 'content' in such attire! But amongst Germans is there not enough to admire, when someone avoids, as Rée has always done, the authentically German devil, the genius or *daimon* of unclarity. The Germans imagine themselves profound."[89] In a similar vein he wrote to his old friend Franz Overbeck, describing the book as poverty-stricken and senile [*altersschwach*].[90] Overbeck replied asking tactfully whether the qualities Nietzsche had previously admired in Rée's work had disappeared.[91] Nietzsche responded with another qualification: "Rée's book, splendidly clear and transparent, gives *me* nothing new, where I expected it;— and for a *historical* demonstration of the old material he lacks the appropriate talent and breadth of knowledge."[92]

In 1886 Nietzsche wrote a new preface to *Human, All-Too-Human*. This is very much a trail-covering exercise in which the generalized figure of the "free spirit" replaces the unnamed source of many of the book's ideas. It concludes with a barely concealed dismissal: "But where today are there psychologists? In France, certainly; perhaps in Russia; definitely not in Germany." However, Nietzsche must have become aware that this statement contrasts strangely with the passage in *Human, All-Too-Human* which places "a German, the author of *Psychological Observations*" alongside La Rochefoucauld and other French moralists. In the following year's preface to *On the Genealogy of Morals*, he takes a more direct approach to the case of Rée.

> The first impulse to publish something of my hypotheses concerning the origin of morality was given me by a clear, tidy, and shrewd, also precocious little book, in which I encountered distinctly for the first time an upside-down and perverse species of genealogical hypothesis, the genuinely *English* type, that attracted me— with the power of attraction which everything contrary, everything antipodal possesses. The title of the little book was *The Origin of the Moral Sensations*; its author Dr Paul Rée; the year of its appearance 1877. Perhaps I have never read anything to which I would have said to myself No, proposition by proposition, conclusion by conclusion, than I did to this book: yet quite without ill-humor or impatience.[93]

There follows a reading of *Human, All-Too-Human* that is dominated by Nietzsche's determination to deny any influence. He allows that his language was similar to Rée's, but claims that it was used to offer alternatives to Rée's propositions; and he lists various passages in *Human, All-Too-Human* and its two sequels in which, he argues, the different approach of *On the Genealogy of Morals* is already present. Furthermore, his intention had been to offer much-needed guidance to Rée. "My wish, at any rate, was to point out to so sharp and disinterested an eye as his a better direction, the direction of an actual *history of morality,* and to warn him in good time against the English practice of making hypotheses in the blue."[94]

After this introduction, the "First Essay" of *On the Genealogy of Morals* opens with a critique of "these English psychologists" who attribute evolution to the inertia of habit, or to forgetfulness, or to some chance combination of ideas. "'Originally'—so they decree—'non-egoistic actions were praised and called good from the point of view of those to whom they were done, that is, to whom they were *useful;* later this origin of praise was *forgotten* and, simply because they were always praised as good *out of habit,* non-egoistic actions were also felt as good—as if they were something good in themselves.'"[95] This is a close summary of the argument of *The Origin of the Moral Sensations,* with the key terms emphasized just as they had been when Nietzsche presented the theory as his own in *The Wanderer and His Shadow.* Having identified the "English" approach to morality, Nietzsche proceeds to state his objections—in effect, presenting for the first time an extended alternative to Rée's approach to morality.

His account of punishment is particularly enlightening, given the prominence of the theme in Rée's work, especially in *The Origin of Conscience.* The previous genealogists of morals, Nietzsche says, have been naive in thinking of punishment as having a "purpose," not only at present but in its distant origins.[96] This is the sort of teleology now banished from biology by the theory of evolution, which no longer regards the eye as made for seeing, or the hand for grasping. Practices, like organs, have a material reality. They result from causes that are quite distinct from the uses later made of them: for "whatever exists, having somehow come into being, is again and again reinterpreted to new ends." Ironically, Nietzsche is being very Darwinian in this objection to Rée's theory.[97] A sequence of adaptations, he points out, is not a "progress" toward some goal but the outcome of contingent situations that have produced corresponding changes.[98] In this case, the process amounts to an accumulation of "meanings." In consequence, punishment as we know it is "overdetermined" by the many utilities that have become attached to it over a long time: "Today it is impossible to say for certain *why* people are punished."

Nietzsche now sketches his own account of the development of "bad conscience."[99] It arose, he says, as an adaptation to a new environment: namely, human society, with its many restrictive laws and sanctions. Under these conditions, the instincts that had been valuable in a state of nature suddenly became dangerous to their owners. They had to be redirected, and since their old outward expressions were now impossible, they were turned *inward*, in a painful process of self-denial and self-negation. In this way arose the concepts of moral guilt and duty, whose further history Nietzsche traces at length, eventually broadening his case into an indictment of European culture as based upon a legacy of hostility to life and "slander" against the world. The book is not headed "A Polemic" [*Eine Streitschrift*] for nothing. Yet Nietzsche's "revaluation of all values" is inseparable from his speculative genealogy of moral concepts, since it identifies values as having the meaning of the forms of life that, on his account, they arise out of and express, in both thought and action.

This is a naturalistic approach that goes well beyond "Réealism." With Rée, valuation is treated as a natural phenomenon, but values are not themselves naturalized. As we saw earlier, his inquiry starts from the conclusions of Schopenhauer's inquiry into the "basis" of morality, which in turn consists largely in a thoroughgoing critique of the legalistic formalism typified in Kant's moral philosophy. For this reason, the philosophical and scientific aspects of Rée's theory are never integrated. Given that he has already accepted Schopenhauer's thesis that moral value is to be identified with selflessness, Rée's naturalism is confined to the task of explaining our moral sense, drawing upon Darwinian biology to provide an alternative to Schopenhauer's dualistic metaphysical doctrine, and thereby vindicating the claim that "moral man stands no closer to the intelligible world than physical man."

Although Nietzsche does not offer a direct "refutation" of Rée's standpoint in *On the Genealogy of Morals,* his own account points to the implied accusation: that the theory of *The Origin of the Moral Sensations* is a rationalization of later attitudes and a misleading projection of these concepts back into a hypothetical past stage of human history. This coincides with Nietzsche's broader judgment on Rée as lacking in "the historical sense."[100] It is significant that in *Beyond Good and Evil* he makes the same charge against Schopenhauer and argues that his influence on subsequent German culture has been harmful in this respect.[101] An insensitivity to other cultures, Nietzsche goes on to argue, may display a certain nobility of taste; but the historical sense gives one "secret access in all directions."[102] What is striking about these judgments on Rée and Schopenhauer is their similarity to the criticisms leveled against existing philosophy in the opening sections of *Human, All-Too-Human.* At that time, Nietzsche had believed that he and Rée could complete the new project of "historical philosophy" together. The later course of their friendship gave him an acute sense of Rée's intellectual limitations and, in particular, of his inability to break away from a set of unquestioned assumptions about morality.[103] Nietzsche still believed in the need to uncover a hidden history of human values, but he now recognized that he would have to undertake this enterprise without the companionship of Paul Rée—or, for that matter, of anyone else.

RÉE'S LATER WRITINGS

A long pause in Rée's publishing activity followed *Psychological Observations* (1875) and *The Origin of the Moral Sensations* (1877), caused largely by the discouragements he encountered in dealing with German universities. In late 1877 he had written to Nietzsche signaling some disagreement over his account of punishment, while reaffirming his basically utilitarian standpoint, and described the new direction of his research into morality:

> The most mistaken thing about my latest work (as you said already, but I did not want to admit—probably because in that case I would have had to revise a lot) is the historical development of punishment (although I still hold that the philosophical view of punishment as merely a means to an end is correct). Now since the most essential mark of a bad act is that it deserves punishment (according to general opinion) a work on the origin of moral consciousness and its history has nothing more important to investigate than precisely the origin of punishment, i.e. it has to investigate the way the belief has developed in human history that certain actions must be followed by suffering and punishment. What we encounter everywhere as a preliminary stage is blood revenge, and to find out about this in various countries, I am studying all the systems of criminal law I can and primitive cultures. In addition, classical antiquity, half in the original language, half in translation.[104]

Work proceeded slowly on this ambitious project, which carried the working title "Prolegomena to a History of Moral Consciousness."[105] Two years later, Rée reported that he had prepared a rough draft, but his determination to add historical content delayed completion still further.[106]

An English book which appeared in 1879, Herbert Spencer's *The Data of Ethics,* covered some of the themes of *The Origin of the Moral Sensations,* but in a very different way. Spencer's argument is structured around the contrast between egoism and altruism.[107] He argues that each is essential to life: egoism to promote the health and fitness of the individual, and altruism to maintain and continue society. Moreover, neither can exist on its own. A pure egoism would be self-defeating, since it would not only alienate others but even dull the sense of pleasure. In some ways, altruism actually serves egoism: for example, we enjoy poetry and art because we sympathize with the feelings of others expressed there. On the other hand, a pure altruism makes no sense, if it implies disapproval of *all* egoistic pleasures—even those which the altruist is trying to promote in others. In any case, the ability to help others depends on the powers that only the "adequately egoistic individual" can maintain: "He who carries self-regard far enough to keep himself in good health and high spirits, in the first place thereby becomes an immediate source of happiness to those around, and in the second place maintains the ability to increase their happiness by altruistic actions."[108] Spencer concludes by advocating a judicious compromise between egoism and altruism, though his opinion is that the greatest sum of happiness is produced if people are, by and large, more egoistic than altruistic. "Hence, beyond the truth that there can be altruistic pleasures there must be the egoistic pleasures from sympathy with which they arise, there is the truth that, in order to obtain the greater sum of altruistic pleasures, there must be a greater sum of egoistic pleasures."[109]

Rée must have read Spencer's discussion, since he refers to it in a later book, noting the argument for an expansion of the parenting instinct through natural selection.[110] But the general outlook of the work would have had no appeal to him. For Spencer, evolution is a steadily improving "adjustment of acts to ends," serving the preservation of the individual and the species, an avoidance of conflict and a promotion of mutual cooperation and assistance. Morality is just those means that serve the general end of promoting pleasure or happiness, having become so complex that they appear as ends in their own right.[111] As society continues to progress, Spencer predicts, altruism will become a marginal phenomenon, primarily taking the form of sympathy with others' pleasures, so that the old conflict between altruism and egoism will be irrelevant.[112] This picture is a long way from Rée's belief in a perennial struggle between egoism and non-egoism, as well as his invariably skeptical and pessimistic assessment of the relationship between moral goodness and happiness.

Not until 1885 did two further books by Rée appear in print. One was a short essay entitled *Die Illusion der Willensfreiheit* [The illusion of free will], spelling out some of the philosophical content of *The Origin of the Moral Sensations* in more detail. To say the will is free, Rée argues, is to say that it is free from causal laws, that an act of will has no sufficient reason. Yet inanimate objects are certainly determined, and so are animals that make choices, such as an ass deciding between two bundles of straw. Unlike the stone, the ass moves because it wants to move, and yet the processes in its brain determine the outcome. So it is with human beings, Rée argues. Every human feeling is the necessary outcome of a series of changes, stretching back into eternity and ruled by causal law. The same goes for all other mental acts, even thinking. "To that extent, there is no freedom of thought. The fact that at this moment I am sitting in this place, holding the pen just so in my hand and writing that every thought is necessary, is necessary; and if the reader harbors the opinion that it is not the case, that thoughts must be treated not as effects, then he has this false opinion just as necessarily."[113]

Actions too are necessary, since they have motives, and therefore causes. Even an energetic "I will" is a necessary product of its causes. Rée illustrates this with an anecdote: "I remember once discussing free will with someone who is left-handed. He asserted, 'My will is free, I can do whatever I want,' and to prove this, he held out his *left* arm."[114] Some choices are so trivial that their determining causes go unremarked, so that we imagine there are none: hence, the illusion of free will. With important, deliberate choices, we see *one* causal factor, but not its combination with many other factors; if we could experiment with varying these, we could figure out how the result came about. As in *The Origin of the Moral Sensations,* Rée claims that someone who accepts determinism will not hold anyone responsible for what are only effects, and insists, "To understand all is to forgive all." Still, we do want to encourage some actions and discourage others, and for this purpose, children are taught that some actions are good and others bad. We make these judgments about ourselves as well, and feel guilty if we have done something wrong. But since character is as much a causal product as any particular act, it is wrong to attribute responsibility even there.

Also published in 1885, *Die Entstehung des Gewissens* [*The Origin of Conscience*] is a much-enlarged version of the theory presented in *The Origin of the Moral Sensations,* including a great deal of anthropological and historical material about the development of moral concepts. About half of the work is concerned with revenge and punishment. Like other writers, Rée presents legal punishment as arising out of revenge. However, his treatment differs from theirs in two ways. For Eugen Dühring, legal justice is no more than "a public administration of revenge."[115] Rée, however, sees it as an alternative to revenge, a utilitarian measure that may happen to satisfy the desire for retribution but which rests on a quite different justification. The second difference is Rée's recognition of an intermediate stage in the process of replacing revenge by punishment, a thesis backed up by numerous references to historical scholarship.

Revenge, as found in primitive cultures, is not to be confused with punishment, understood as an expression of the sentiment of justice, so that historians who run the two together are mistaken. Rée continues to follow Schopenhauer in holding that what motivates revenge is the feeling of inferiority. "The sweetness of revenge is thus something negative, namely the elimination of the pain of inferiority."[116] And this is not necessarily linked with injustice: we can want to take out our sufferings on others without feeling that we have been unfairly treated by them. Revenge is egoistic (we "revenge ourselves") whereas justice is impersonal. The next stage of development is a substitution of payment for revenge. In traditional cultures, even murder can be paid off by the perpetrator. Societies formalize this procedure by recognizing places of asylum to prevent vengeance, and by fixing a standard price for expiating each type of offence. The state mediates the dispute and guarantees the validity of the settlement. With punishment, the payment is at first to the aggrieved party rather than to the state for its contribution. "Later, the state becomes the central figure. More weight is placed on payment to the state, because the wrongdoer has to suffer, than on reconciliation with the aggrieved victim."[117] The offender who has broken the peace owes a debt to society. More importantly, the state wants to prevent such acts. Monetary penalties are not a sufficient deterrent, and so punishment is needed as a practical measure. This brings with it an emphasis on preventing deliberate wrongdoing, since that is the object of deterrence. Hence, the distinction between deliberate and nondeliberate offences is now made for the first time.

After this long historical survey, Rée turns his attention to the development of conscience in the individual person. The account is very similar to *The Origin of the Moral Sensations,* but since Rée is now concerned to establish academic credentials by a display of scholarship, he acknowledges an indebtedness to the jurist Paul Johann Anselm Feuerbach's earlier theory of punishment. Feuerbach had made the crucial distinction between punishment [*Strafe*] and discipline [*Züchtigung*]. The aim of discipline is to guide future behavior, not only preventing wrongful actions but encouraging desirable ones. While it is carried out only after some breach, that behavior is only the "occasion" of the disciplinary action, Feuerbach says, and not its real reason. In contrast, punishment is not concerned with any improvement of offenders: hence, it is appropriate even where no improvement is possible. Many people have confused punishment and discipline, he notes, and even attempted an impossible combination of the concepts. Feuerbach locates the source of the mistake in the practice of upbringing. The disciplining of children *seems* to refer only to their past behavior, although it is in fact directed toward the future.[118] As an aspect of education, its aim is to make children not just law-abiding, but ethical: that is, in the end they must freely choose to do what is right. This is why a moral vocabulary is used—so that immorality will come to have painful associations for the child. This practice, however, makes discipline seem to be punishment, and indeed it is even called punishment, although that is strictly a misuse of language.

In ways like this, *The Origin of Conscience* throws light on Rée's earlier theory without adding much in the way of new ideas. As a British reviewer observed, "it is rather noticeable for what it omits of the pessimism of the earlier book, for a more moderate, thoughtful, and less assertive tone, than for additional theories or even much further elaboration of the old theories, except as regards the derivation of the Sense of Justice."[119] This lack of progress is also seen in Rée's final book, which was published only after his death. Simply entitled *Philosophie,* it is prefaced by a formal retraction of his previous works: "My earlier writings are immature works of youth." Yet the new book is just a restatement of his earlier ideas: Rée's views on ethics and metaphysics have not developed at all. *Philosophie* begins with essays on the origin of conscience and on vanity which repeat his previous accounts, often word for word. They are followed by a general survey of metaphysics that expresses a strong preference for the skeptical side of British empiricism. "The greatest philosophers are Berkeley and Hume," Rée announces. For Berkeley shows that matter has no reality apart from our ideas, and Hume proves that cause and effect have no necessary connection.[120] In contrast, the book's discussion of Kant is very hostile, while Schopenhauer is described as a good observer and sometimes brilliant writer but lacking the philosophical ability of the British thinkers. Echoing an earlier thesis, Rée writes, "The most fundamental of Schopenhauer's fundamental errors is his assertion that moral man belongs to a different world-order from physical man."[121]

Rée's style is by now curt and dogmatic rather than aphoristic, although he is still capable of the occasional phrase ("Opinions are upheld most obstinately by those who have none"). More disturbing is the extent to which *Philosophie* is haunted by the specter of Nietzsche. Its format, a sequence of aphorisms and short paragraphs, each with a number and even a title, is that of *Human, All-Too-Human, Daybreak* and *The Gay Science* rather than of Rée's earlier essays. It is hard to see this as other than an eloquent testimony to a preoccupation with his onetime and now-famous friend. In an appendix to *Philosophie,* an anonymous editor includes an extract from a letter written in 1897, which contains Rée's last, bitter verdict on Nietzsche, in the form of comments made on a recently published essay on Carlyle and Nietzsche by J. H. Wilhelmi. "I am in the middle of Wilhelmi's book, which is good. His presentation is simple, clear and capable. And I am getting to know Nietzsche for the first time; *but I have never been able to read him.* He is rich in spirit and poor in thought. If you reduce the quotations collected by Wilhelmi to their sheer thought content, you get scarcely a grain. This selection puts me off reading him. He is very enjoyable (a crazy poet?) in a capable selection like Wilhelmi's, but not taken together. His moral thought is a mixture of insanity and nonsense. Wilhelmi gives a clear and accurate picture of the person and the theory."[122]

Rée's judgment on this book is a reasonable assessment. Wilhelmi argues that both Carlyle and Nietzsche were driven by a strong religious inclination and that, although they rejected conventional religion, both found it impossible to live according to a materialist philosophy which eliminated meaning and value from the world.[123] Wilhelmi's reading of Nietzsche as a frustrated God-seeker contains a certain amount of special pleading in favor of his own faith, but he shows fair-mindedness in arguing that Nietzsche's ideas should be taken seriously, despite the fact of his mental breakdown, and he even suggests that they identify the important issues for modern Christianity. The book includes many short quotations from Nietzsche, nearly all taken from the later books and arranged according to themes in a similar way to other selections from his writing. If Rée's comments on Nietzsche are addressed to these passages rather than to his earlier work, his statement "I have never been able to read him" is perhaps not as absurd as one might suppose. The prophetic manner and dithyrambic style of the later Nietzsche would not have appealed to the author of *The Origin of the Moral Sensations.* Nor for that matter would his intention to undermine the ideals of scientific rationalism and utilitarianism to which Rée remained committed to the end of his life.

Rée's career in philosophy ended in frustration and disappointment, yet in part this was the result of his own limitations. The ideas presented in his youthful work were never developed further, or even expressed better, in his later writings, but only repeated with minor variations and supplemented with historical scholarship—which, however, tends to figure as illustration rather than supporting evidence. Rée remained a pure philosopher, despite his ambition to find scientific solutions to the problems of moral theory. On a personal level, it was Rée's fate to see his efforts overtaken by others—and very close at hand. His talent for the aphorism was surpassed by Friedrich Nietzsche in *Human, All-Too-Human* and its various sequels, and his program for an evolutionary ethics was carried out with greater public recognition by Herbert Spencer in *The Data of Ethics.* Even when Rée finally brought out his major scholarly production, *The Origin of Conscience,* the attention of the German reading public was drawn instead to Lou Salomé's novel *Im Kampf um Gott,* which appeared at the same time.

Despite all this, there are several reasons for returning to Rée's early writings. The relation of his ideas to Nietzsche's has been obscured by the partial and distorted account presented in the prefaces that Nietzsche added to his early books after his break with Rée. Only by comparing *Psychological Observations* and *The Origin of the Moral Sensations* directly with works such as *Human, All-Too-Human* can we appreciate the degree of revisionism in these intellectual autobiographies. What about Rée's interest in his own right? He is a genuine pioneer in evolutionary ethics, a century before the emergence of sociobiology, who rightly identifies the problem of altruism that has been central to so much recent debate. Further, he goes beyond the origin of altruistic behavior to the question of its moral interpretation and, in so doing, addresses a problem that Darwin had overlooked in his own discussion of the moral sense. The defect of Rée's evolutionary ethics, his uncritical use of a simple principle of group selection, was shared by other evolutionary theorists, both at that time and for many years afterward, so that our recognition of its inadequacy owes much to hindsight. Finally, there is an enduring quality that even Nietzsche continued to appreciate and praise after his personal rift with Rée: the clear and objective prose style that is so unlike that of much German philosophy of his time and which, as readers of this volume can judge for themselves, makes him as readable as ever, a hundred years after his death.

NOTES

1. Nietzsche, letter of 22 October 1875, *Kritische Gesamtausgabe: Briefwechsel* [hereafter KGB] II/5 [Division 2, volume 5], 122–23.

2. Letter of 31 October 1875, KGB II/6/1 [Division 2, volume 6, part 1], 249.

3. Rée later told Ferdinand Tönnies that Nietzsche was much more important in his letters than in his books, and more important again in conversation than in letters. Tönnies, "Paul Rée," 670.

4. Letter of 25 December 1876 in Pfeiffer, *Friedrich Nietzsche*, 20.

5. Letter of 20 February 1877 in ibid., 24.

6. Letter of 16 June 1888, KGB II/5, 33.

7. Letter of June 1877, KGB II/5, 245–46.

8. Letter of 3–4 August 1877, KGB II/5, 265–66.

9. See letter of 20 September 1877, KGB II/6/2, 702.

10. Review of Paul Rée, *Der Ursprung*, 581.

11. Letter of 30 December 1877, KGB II/6/2, 786.

12. Letter of 19 October 1879, KGB II/6/2, 1194.

13. Letter of Summer 1880, KGB III/2, 100.

14. Letter of 27 March 1882, KGB III/2, 247–48.

15. Andreas-Salomé, *Looking Back*, 48.

16. Letter of 14–15 June 1882 in Pfeiffer, *Friedrich Nietzsche*, 144. Nietzsche's reaction was: "Oh the bad photographer! And yet—what a lovely silhouette is sitting on the little cart!" Letter of 28 May 1882 in ibid., 126.

17. Allison, *Reading the New Nietzsche*, 155. For a contrasting analysis of the episode, see Diethe, *Nietzsche's Women*, 49–61.

18. See Treiber, "Paul Rée," 46.

19. Rée's aphorisms were not numbered in the original edition of *Psychologische Beobachtungen*. Numbers have been added in this translation to enable easier reference.

20. One chapter of Schopenhauer's *Parerga and Paralipomena* is headed "Psychological Remarks," presumably the model for Rée's title.

21. Darwin, *Works*, 15:150.

22. Ibid., 22:384.

23. Schopenhauer, *On the Basis of Morality*, sect. 13, 130.

24. Ibid., sect. 15, 139.

25. Ibid., sect. 22, 204.

26. Darwin, *Works*, 21:127. The full text is in Bain, *Mental and Moral Science*, 722.

27. Spencer, *Social Statics*, 57.

28. Ibid., 64. Nietzsche's criticisms of Spencer in his notebooks are often aimed at these claims; see, e.g., Nietzsche, *Kritische Gesamtausgabe: Werke* [hereafter KGW], VIII/2, 204, and VIII/3, 34 (*The Will to Power*, sect. 541).

29. Spencer, "Progress," 447. Spencer then proceeds to identify an underlying reason for such a universal pattern: "Every active force produces more than one change—every cause produces more than one effect." Ibid., 466.

30. See, e.g., Darwin, *Works*, 15:240, 314, 338.

31. Schopenhauer, *On the Basis of Morality*, sect. 3, 51.

32. See, e.g., Spencer, *The Data of Ethics*, 190–91.

33. Dennett, *Darwin's Dangerous Idea*, 466.

34. Darwin, *Works*, 21:130.

35. Ibid., 21:79.

36. Ibid., 21:112.

37. Ibid., 21:123.

38. Ibid., 21:124.

39. Ibid., 21:115.

40. Ibid., 21:123.

41. Ibid., 21:137.

42. Ibid., 21:127–28.

43. Ibid., 22:636.

44. Ibid., 21:118.

45. Ibid., 21:129.

46. Rée, *Entstehung des Gewissens*, 219.

47. Darwin, *Works*, 21:137.

48. Ibid., 22:643.

49. Ibid., 15:55–56.

50. Even the *proportion* of altruists in the overall population may increase, surprising though this may seem, given their disadvantage within each particular group. See Sober and Wilson, *Unto Others*, 23–26.

51. Darwin, *Works*, 15:62.

52. Trivers, "Evolution of Reciprocal Altruism," 35.

53. Ibid., 47–54; see also Axelrod, *Evolution of Co-operation*.

54. It would have to be for at least two siblings to achieve a genetic profit, since only

half of the individual's genes are shared by each sibling. See Hamilton, "Evolution of Altruistic Behavior," 355.

55. Jaspers, *Nietzsche*, 73.

56. Letter of 24 April 1878, KGB II/5, 324.

57. Nietzsche, *Human, All-Too-Human*, sect. 35. In quoting from the published writings of Nietzsche, and from the notes included in *The Will to Power,* the translations of Walter Kaufmann and R. J. Hollingdale have been used, with some modifications. Section numbers have been given in order to enable reference to any edition.

58. A notebook entry of early 1877 reads: "Describe Rée as a skilful marksman who always hits the black circle." KGW IV/2, 517.

59. Nietzsche, *Human, All-Too-Human*, sect. 37.

60. The "metaphysical need" is posited by Schopenhauer; see *World as Will and Representation,* 2:160–87.

61. Nietzsche, *Human, All-Too-Human*, sect. 39 and 89.

62. Ibid., sect. 70.

63. Ibid., sect. 302.

64. Rée, *Psychological Observations*, sect. 226.

65. Nietzsche, *Wanderer and His Shadow*, sect. 40.

66. Ibid., sect. 45.

67. KGW IV/1, 355.

68. A subtle discussion of this theme can be found in Babich, *Nietzsche's Philosophy of Science,* 15–32.

69. Nietzsche, *Genealogy of Morals,* preface, sect. 8.

70. Nietzsche, *Wanderer and His Shadow,* sect. 55.

71. Letter of 20 November 1879 in Pfeiffer, *Friedrich Nietzsche,* 70.

72. Schaberg, *Nietzsche Canon,* 59. The source for this text is Elisabeth Förster-Nietzsche, not always a reliable authority; but it is consistent with other evidence, such as the drafted letter cited below.

73. Letter of 25 January 1878, KGB II/6/2, 796.

74. Letter of 28 January 1878, KGB II/5, 301.

75. KGB II/5, 298–99. The drafted letter was apparently intended to accompany a copy of the new book but was set aside following Schmeitzner's negative response.

76. Entry for 25 April 1878, Wagner, *Diaries,* 2:65.

77. See, e.g., Nietzsche, *Human, All-Too-Human,* sect. 146, 147, 222.

78. Hayman, *Nietzsche,* 204.

79. Entry for 24 June 1878, Wagner, *Diaries,* 2:100.

80. Letter of 31 May 1878, KGB II/5, 329.

81. Wagner, *Prose Works,* 6:78. Cf. *Human, All-Too-Human,* sect. 113: "When on Sunday we hear the bells ringing we ask ourselves: is it possible! this is going on because of a Jew crucified two thousand years ago, who said he was the son of God."

82. Letter of 25 August 1878, KGB II/5, 347.

83. Letter of 16 June 1878, KGB II/5, 333. The reference to "conception" looks like an

uneasy echo of Rée's dedication in the copy of *Der Ursprung der moralischen Empfin-dungen* he gave to Nietzsche.

84. Letter of 10 August 1878, KGB II/5, 347.

85. Publisher's announcement at the end of Dühring, *Robert Mayer.*

86. Nietzsche, *Daybreak,* sect. 103.

87. Tönnies, "Paul Rée," 670.

88. Letters of 6 March and 17 April 1883, KGB III/1, 339, 360.

89. Letter of 15 October 1885, KGB III/3, 100.

90. Letter of 17 October 1885, KGB III/3, 102.

91. Letter of 29 November 1885, KGB III/4, 85.

92. Letter of December 1885, KGB III/3, 118.

93. Nietzsche, *Genealogy of Morals,* preface, sect. 4.

94. Ibid., sect. 7. A similar claim is made in Nietzsche, *Gay Science,* sect. 345.

95. Nietzsche, *Genealogy of Morals,* First Essay, sect. 2.

96. Ibid., Second Essay, sect. 12.

97. His argument owes a good deal to a reading of Rolph, *Biologische Probleme.* See Moore, *Nietzsche, Biology, and Metaphor,* 47–55, for an insightful discussion of Rolph's ideas and Nietzsche's response to them.

98. At the same time, Nietzsche introduces the un-Darwinian "will to power" into these processes, in order to avoid what he thinks is a misunderstanding of life as "a mere reactivity."

99. Nietzsche, *Genealogy of Morals,* Second Essay, sect. 16.

100. KGW VII/1, 529, and VII/3, 247.

101. Nietzsche, *Beyond Good and Evil,* sect. 204.

102. Ibid., sect. 224.

103. Paul-Laurent Assoun suggests that Nietzsche came to see Rée much as Sigmund Freud came to see Josef Breuer a few years later: that is, as a discoverer who backed away from the implications of his insights. Assoun, "Nietzsche," 62–64.

104. Letter of 10 October 1877, KGB II/6/2, 717–18.

105. Letters of early June and 2 July 1877, KGB II/6/1, 582, 596.

106. Letter of 19 October 1879, KGB II/6/2, 1194–95.

107. The term "altruism" [*altruisme*] had been coined by Auguste Comte as a counterpart to "egoism."

108. Spencer, *Data of Ethics,* 193.

109. Ibid., 229.

110. Rée, *Entstehung des Gewissens,* 240.

111. Spencer, *Data of Ethics,* 162.

112. Ibid., 255.

113. Rée, *Illusion der Willensfreiheit,* 9.

114. Ibid., 16.

115. See Small, *Nietzsche in Context,* 172–74, for a fuller discussion of Dühring's account.

116. Rée, *Entstehung des Gewissens,* 41.

117. Ibid., 103.

118. Feuerbach, *Revision der Grundsätze,* 1:18. This passage is quoted with minor changes by Rée in *Entstehung des Gewissens,* 192.

119. Williams, *Review of the Systems of Ethics,* 267.

120. Rée, *Philosophie,* 244. These were not new ideas: many years earlier, Rée had told Nietzsche that he was writing a defense of Hume's empiricist theory of causality. Letter of 10 October 1877, KGB II/6/2, 718.

121. Rée, *Philosophie,* 321.

122. Ibid., 362.

123. Wilhelmi, *Carlyle und Nietzsche,* 19.

PART 1

Psychological Observations

From the *Nachlass* of ⁎⁎⁎

L'homme est l'animal méchant par excellence."[1]

Some read to improve their hearts, others to improve their minds: I write for the latter.

CONTENTS

On Books and Authors

1

Aphorisms are a thought concentrate that anyone can expand for themselves according to their taste.

Such a writing style is to be recommended. In the first place, it is not very easy to express a real stupidity in a short, pithy way. For it cannot hide itself behind few words nearly as well as behind many. In any case, the great quantity of literature makes a short mode of expression desirable.

2

The value of an aphorism cannot be judged by its author until he has forgotten the concrete cases from which it has been abstracted.

3

The fact that the author proceeds from the individual to the general, and the reader from the general to the individual, is the source of numerous misunderstandings between them.

4

Vauvenargues says, "If the illustrious author of the *Maxims* had been such as he tried to depict everyone, would he have deserved our respect and the idolatrous cult of his followers?"[2]

This question is absurd: for what La Rochefoucauld's followers admire is not the goodness of his heart, but the subtlety of his head.

5

That a person's goodness consists in the degree of his disinterested concern for the fate of others, and his practical rationality in not following momentary inclinations but taking the future into account, and that every person ought to be good and rational, everyone knows from himself and does not need to learn from moral philosophy.

Moreover, since the extent of our goodness, as much as of our rationality, depends mainly on our inborn nature, and in the second place on whether we had frequent opportunities from youth onward for the pursuit of good and rational actions, whereas reading the philosophers achieves nothing—it follows that philosophy (and similarly art) cannot exist for moral goals. Rather, it serves for the conversation and intellectual edification of those who have a natural interest in such matters.

6

The most important author has the smallest public.

7

We see every great author at the first stage of his career surrounded by critics who bark at him, as village dogs bark at a traveler to keep him away. Yet the dogs eventually return to their village, and the critics to the state of obscurity that they needlessly left for a moment.

8

Great models are useful only for great successors.

9

Speakers and authors generally convince only those who were already convinced.

10

When we read a respected author, we revise our judgment according to him.

On the other hand, when we read an author who is not yet respected, we revise him according to our judgment.

Hence, a famous author can receive credit for his bad books more easily than an unknown author for his good ones.

11

Scholars shine, like the moon, with reflected light.

12

The philologist knows books just as accurately as the paper they are printed on knows them.

13

We are not always pleased when someone agrees with our favorable judgment on a great man. For we are so vain that we want to be the only one qualified to appreciate him.

14

The brain of many is pickled in scholarship.

15

The "bookworm" finds pleasure in study itself, not in the things studied.

16

The mere scholar is more conceited than the philosopher. For the philosopher often finds that things he has reflected on for years are better known to the naïve and perhaps uneducated person than to him, whereas of all the things that the scholar knows, no uneducated person has the slightest inkling.

17

What is found in histories of philosophy is either the same as in the philosophers—in which case the histories are useless; or else different—in which case they are harmful.

18

If vanity did not exist, nearly all the sciences would still be in the cradle.

19

Someone who has understood the masterpieces of poetry will seldom take pleasure in holding forth about them, feeling that the beauties of such works cannot be communicated by words to those who do not feel them immediately in reading the works themselves.

Hence, one must have understood the poets very little to be able to write a history of literature.

20

How badly many books would stand up to our critical judgment, if we had not written them ourselves.

21

When facts stand in contradiction with our system, we do not admit them to ourselves.

22

We regard only those critics as competent who praise our achievements.

23

Newly discovered truths are opposed partly out of envy toward their teacher and partly to avoid admitting that one was mistaken for so long.

24

The author is seldom satisfied with the public. For while he sees the beauties of his work and feels its weaknesses only faintly, the public does the opposite, to his astonishment.

25

Human insights are like small islands that float about, lonely, in the infinite sea of our ignorance.

26

It is not in the nature of things probable that the praise people give to our achievements comes closer to the truth than the blame. Nevertheless, we always hold the former to be true and the latter to be untrue.

27

The thought never occurs to us that someone does not understand what he is saying, and yet we should have experienced in our own case how often this is true.

28

A fool fills his traveling flask with water from a Swiss puddle, brings it home, and says, "Look, this is what the water of the Swiss lakes looks like"—and people believe him.

So it has been for the Germans with French literature.

29

If the so-called unities of Aristotle are heavy fetters for the dramatist, one must admit that the French dramatists know how to move in those fetters with great grace and skill.[3]

30

Whoever is eminent within his profession appears to himself to be eminent in general; it does not occur to him that other professions stand much higher than his.

31

It is remarkable how people take a lively interest in an unpublished poem by Goethe or Schiller, even when they know only a minute amount of the published work.

32

Any system is found correct in all its aspects only by its founder.

33

When one has once changed one's opinions, there arises, as with second love, a feeling of uncertainty and mistrust of one's own constancy.

34

The fact that everyone else also holds their opinion to be correct should make us mistrustful of the correctness of our opinion.

35

Stupid people achieve office and status quickly because no talent distracts them from their occupation.

36

To recognize that the good things of this world do not make one happy is difficult, almost impossible, before one possesses them; but then everyone recognizes this truth. Hence, the writings of the moral philosophers on this subject cannot have a practical goal.

37

Geniuses make an impression on the commonplace person only when they show some knowledge of his own daily occupation.

38

With average aptitude one gets on in the world more easily than with extraordinary talents.

39

Insignificant people, who have only weak sides, should not criticize the weaknesses of important people.

40

Whoever asserts that there are no inborn talents is usually right in his own case.

41

The fable of the wren who flew even higher than the eagle under whose wings he had risen so far is especially valid for many a writer who has gone one step beyond his predecessor.[4]

42

The maxim of Vauvenargues "Fools do not understand men of talent" is also correct the other way around: Men of talent do not understand fools.[5]

43

The fact that someone does not know some scientific fact is incomprehensible to us, even if we ourselves have learned it just half an hour earlier.

44

It has been asserted that an author is in the wrong when he describes human misery—since this makes people even more unhappy. But that is a mistake. For what is especially painful to the unhappy person is that he himself is unhappy whereas so many other people are happy.

If he now comes to see that all advantages of gifts, status and possession have their compensating sufferings, that in the end nobody is happy, that unhappiness is rather an integral component of human life, this insight will contribute much more to an alleviation than to an increase of his own suffering.

On Human Actions and Their Motives

45

Observing the motives for his behavior is useless for the practical person, indeed disturbing and harmful to his activity, but very useful for the theoretical person.

46

Every action arises out of a mosaic of motives without our being able to tell from how much egoism, vanity, pride, fear, benevolence, etc., it is composed. The philosopher cannot, like the chemist, apply a quantitative and qualitative analysis to the case.

In any case, the expressions "egoism," "vanity," etc., do not at all coincide with the feelings they indicate; they are really only pointers.

47

We usually think our actions are determined by our principles, when in fact our principles are determined by our actions.

48

The motives of our most splendid acts often resemble those substances from which white paper is made.

49

Our moral behavior depends on our will; our moral character, in contrast, (the goodness and badness of our heart) does not depend on our will. Accordingly, our moral behavior can be improved by experience and instruction, but our moral character is constant.

50

Our attentions to others, which seem to be the direct expression of our affection and goodness, are always the result of a deliberation that goes into the smallest detail.

51

One admits one's stupidities to show that one is clever enough to be aware of them.

52

We complain that we have been made hard and bad by the world to encourage the belief that we are innately good.

53

Nobody is completely sincere toward himself; and most people have a real talent for insincerity.

54

There do not exist two people whose intimacy would not suffer from a completely unreserved openness.

55

To him who has shall be given, since he can give back.[6]

56

Whoever comes to the defense of his friends is usually only defending his own honor in being their friend.

57

Our actions are guided by the opinion of the world. Hence, even with things that concern ourselves exclusively, we do not so much what seems good to us as what seems good to others.

58

Whether we take people in general to be good or bad depends on our philosophy. But in the conduct of life, we constantly take them to be good if we ourselves are good, and to be bad if we ourselves are bad.

59

The end always justifies the means when the well-being of many can be achieved only through the suffering of a few.

On this also rests the right and the necessity of punishment.

60

"He does not understand people," that is, he takes them to be good.

61

Accidents occurring to others, which we recount in order to produce astonishment, are never great enough for us, and so we usually take it upon ourselves to add a few more burned or crushed or drowned or poisoned victims.

62

By our good deeds we want to surprise and astonish.

Hence, we prefer to give to those who have not asked us, and if we give something to the same person a second or third time, it is much less gladly than the first time, for just this reason.

If one wants to receive good deeds from someone more often, one must display the greatest surprise and a boundless gratitude on each occasion. For in this way one encourages the giver to continue, since he goes on expecting the same mood.

63

The benefactor imagines that the recipient, charmed by him, cries out, "What a divinely good person," and indeed he sheds tears over the greatness of his own benevolence.

64

The purpose of personal familiarity is neither to gather advice nor to lessen cares: one wants to be charmed by the other.

65

"We will see each other again before my departure," one says, knowing very well that one will not see the other again. This happens sometimes to spare oneself the pain of parting, but usually to spare oneself the affectation of the pain of parting.

66

Everyone condemns flatterers, but no one can do without them.

67

Teaching alters our behavior, not our character.

68

Anyone who believes he has become morally better is usually only admitting his badness to himself less than before.

69

The person who sticks obstinately to a decision once it is made does so less from strength of character than because he has said that he always sticks to a decision.

70

Many a person believes himself not to be envious because he has had no occasion to feel envy.

71

Our envy is always greater than the good fortune of those we envy.

72

When we say something bad about someone, we like to precede it with some praise, so that people will take us for impartial and believe what follows all the more.

73

Our interest is not as sensitive as our vanity.

74

At a masked ball, one involuntarily reasons from a beautiful mask to a beautiful face, and in life one involuntarily reasons from friendly behavior to a friendly character.

75

We always condemn the criminal too harshly. For we feel only the enormity of his deed, but not the passionate state out of which it emerged.

76

Our dissatisfaction with the world commonly arises from its dissatisfaction with us.

77

We always treat our own guilt for some physical or moral evil as part of a chain of causes and effects, but the guilt of others, in contrast, as a point of origin.

78

Anyone who finds the behavior of someone else senseless sees the standpoint from which the other has decided only in part, or does not take into account the difference of his character.

79

We always infer from ourselves to others, that is, we attribute to others the motives from which we ourselves are in the habit of acting. But this inference occurs so immediately and involuntarily that we nevertheless do not come to know our inner selves and have no inkling at all that we have inferred from our own motives to their motives.

80

One laughs wholeheartedly only at one's own jokes.

81

We excuse people all their good qualities, except for those by which we ourselves want to shine.

82

We excuse people their failings, but not their knowledge of our failings.

83

The inference from bad actions to a bad character is more certain than the inference from good actions to a good character.

84

When someone has succeeded, we immediately ask about how he managed it, in the hope of attributing as much as possible to circumstances and luck, and as little as possible to his personal contribution.

Whoever wants to annoy someone else with his success, accordingly recounts the mere fact and keeps quiet about the contributing circumstances.

85

Good morals are a constraint that one imposes on oneself out of fear of sickness or punishment or disgrace.

86

The moral customs of peoples are more diverse than their moral characters.

87

Since the egoism of the crowd is held in check less by fear of punishment than by fear of disgrace (sense of honor) and since rulers and their officials are impelled to maintain strict law and order less by a sense of duty and calling than by vanity (ambition and sense of honor), it follows that, other things being equal, a civil society would probably not be possible without the existence of vanity.

88

When we are pleased by harm occurring to others, this occurs:

Either, because their unhappiness recalls our happiness, their poverty recalls our wealth (explanation of malicious pleasure [*Schadenfreude*] by association of ideas, according to Lucretius).[7] This malicious pleasure arising through selfishness is seldom very strong.

Or, since their harm gives us the feeling of dominance, of superiority. This malicious pleasure arising through vanity is usually very strong, and on it is based the proverb "There is no need to add insult to injury."[8]

The malicious pleasure of women and children is all the more intense, in that they are only relatively seldom able to enjoy the feeling of dominance.

89

The deepest malicious pleasure is that which follows a previous feeling of envy.

90

We do not judge someone's actions objectively, but rather interpret them in a good or bad sense according to the good or bad opinion that we already have of him.

91

Instead of saying "He is proud, egoistic, vain," it would be more accurate to say, "We can see his pride, his egoism, his vanity."

92

We experience the motives of our own actions as seldom as the motives of others' actions.

93

Our vanity does not tolerate the fact that we find a famous writer boring, or do anything at all that is disapproved of in our time and in our social position. Hence, the almost complete uniformity in the actions and judgments of people, despite the great diversity of moral sensations and intellectual impressions.

94

Betrayals of us make us so angry because they mock our power of judgment.

95

We regret our base actions less intensely then our lapses in etiquette.

96

We display to those around us an abhorrence of lying, partly out of fear of being lied to and partly to gain credit for our own love of truth.

97

Often one speaks the truth out of lack of presence of mind.

98

Whether we find someone friendly depends less on the impression he has made on us than on the impression we think we have made on him.

99

In life it is often a question of who best understands how to annoy the other.

100

It lies in human nature to think: Hate me, but admire me.

101

One would rather be distinguished before other people by vices than not be distinguished before them at all.

102

Relatives are more uncharitable toward each other than strangers.

103

Weaklings do evil and imagine they are good. Strong natures admit to themselves the evil that they do.

104

We grieve over the death of relatives as long and as deeply as is seemly.

105

Nowhere are we as modest as where our good qualities are recognized and known to the greatest extent.

106

The tenderness we bestow on someone is often due to another person whom we want to annoy.

107

In order to console ourselves about someone's intellectual merits, we happily attribute many moral faults to him.

108

Punished children cry less from pain than in order to annoy or worry the person punishing them.

109

The modest person wants to add the reputation of friendliness to that of greatness.

110

The educator should reflect that many fruits taste good to us just because they are forbidden. Accordingly, when children are supposed not to do something, they should merely give the children full permission to do it.

Similarly, the unfaithfulness of many wives is merely a consequence of the mistrustful strictness with which the husband controls all their movements.

111

Who can fail to be consoled over the death of a famous friend, when one has a beautiful and sensitive funeral address on him already prepared?

112

Children are more uncharitable to one another than adults, since they pretend less to one another.

113

We praise the modesty of a great man in gratitude for his not injuring our pride.

114

Many are vain in their lack of vanity.

115

The fantasies of the ambitious person always feature people who are annoyed over his success.

116

Someone approached by a beggar on a public street often cannot help feeling that he must appear more fashionable and generous than the rest, and this flattering feeling is not seldom the only motive for his beneficence.

117

Usually we hate a person not so much because of the actual suffering he has caused us, but because we have been made to feel his power and superiority, in addition to the suffering.[9]

Accordingly, the satisfaction of revenge is based on the fact that we have made our power felt by the hated person.

118

We are sometimes annoyed when someone congratulates us on our success with sincere cordiality: we wanted to be envied specifically by him.

119

Someone who feels he has been tactless toward us does not forgive us for that.

120

Children who care for their sick parents leave nothing undone to quieten their conscience, but in secret they wish that the death of the parents might soon free them from their duty.

121

One humbles oneself because one thinks: He that humbles himself shall be exalted.[10]

122

In one respect we sincerely hold others to be better than ourselves: the thought never occurs to us that they speak just as badly about us as we speak about them.

123

Anyone who has achieved something outstanding arouses the strongest envy in his own home country. For the companions of his youth feel his eminence most clearly and painfully, since they once stood alongside him. Hence, they belittle his merits as much as possible to relieve their envy, whereas the envied person is very happy to display his merits in his home country, precisely because of arousing this strong envy.

124

We allow our friends as much tenderness and support as we believe they might know to be present in our hearts.

125

We like to treat our failings as typical of the human race ("Everyone is like that," "Everyone does that"). In this way, the failing admittedly does not cease to be a failing, but we no longer need to regard others as better than ourselves.

126

Only seldom do the sufferings of others distress us for longer than we observe them.

127

Base actions are performed with the greatest self-assurance by those who never admit their baseness to themselves.

128

We often imagine others as bad in order not to have to despise ourselves in comparison with them.

129

One displays sympathy in order to be taken as a sympathetic person.

130

Despite our general falseness toward others, we take their friendliness toward us to be sincere.

131

Our friends are often less pleased by the good aspects of our work than by its bad aspects.

132

We are envious of the advantages of another either because they are pleasant in their own right (e.g., health) or because the other is favored, admired, or envied on their account (e.g., beauty, rank).

The *first* feeling of envy we admit straight away. For it arises from a natural and permissible self-interest. Also, we do not at all want the other to lose his advantage; we would simply like to possess a similar advantage as well.

The *second* feeling of envy, in contrast, we do not admit. For it springs from vanity. We wish not only to possess the same kind of advantages but also that the envied person may lose his distinguishing advantage.

Most feelings of envy arise not out of self-interest, but out of vanity.

Further, envy out of self-interest is never as strong and painful as envy out of vanity.

Conversely, when someone is envious of those of our advantages that are pleasant in their own right, this feeling of envy is certainly pleasing to us, because it reminds us of the possession and value of those advantages; but when someone is envious of those advantages on account of which we are favored and admired, or when someone is simply envious of the fact that we are favored and admired, this feeling of envy is all the more pleasant to us; for it flatters our vanity.

133

If our envy arose from self-interest, we would envy the happy and contented; but since it arises mainly out of vanity, we envy the famous, respected, and rich.

134

Envy depends on the semblance of happiness.

135

We tell our friends that their unhappiness is less than it is, less to give them comfort than to relieve ourselves from the trouble of comforting them.

136

Hatred and antipathy are different in kind.

Hatred refers to a single fact, antipathy is directed toward the whole nature of a person, against his mode of being.

Out of antipathy there often develops a state of irritation in consequence of which every word of a person, the tone of his voice, and every one of his actions are unpleasant to us and make us hostile to him.

Many women, especially older ones, are disposed toward their husbands in this way.

Conversely, with someone who is wholly sympathetic to us, we find even the repulsive things he does not unpleasant.

We do not like to admit to ourselves and others that we hate someone, partly because hatred is a far from benevolent feeling, and partly because we do not want to admit that someone has sufficient power over us to arouse our hatred by means of insult, jealousy, or unrequited love.

Therefore, hatred is often passed off as antipathy.

On the other hand, those to whom people are merely unsympathetic are commonly designated as haters of humanity (misanthropes).

Further, since the hated person has made others feel his power, he finds more that is flattering to him than is annoying in the hater through whom his power is confirmed. The commandment "Love those who hate you" is thus easy to obey.[11]

137

The reconciliation of two enemies is commonly brought about by their common hatred for a third person.

138

When two persons feel wholly sympathetic to each other, their unsympathetic sides have not yet emerged.

139

In our choice of company, our sympathy is less decisive than our vanity.

140

The moral behavior of a people may be strongly influenced by chance occurrences, such as the appearance of an outstanding ruler. For everyone is careful not to do what would be disapproved of by the persons or circles who set the tone. But at the bottom of their hearts, they all remain as bad and selfish as they were.

141

A person who is usually impudent and overbearing charms the whole world if he shows himself to be modest just once.

On the other hand, if a normally modest person behaves impudently just once, people almost believe that he has gone mad.

Therefore it is not unwise to make a habit of being impudent. Admittedly, that must differ according to character: it suits one person to be impudent, another, to be modest.

142

The person of high rank knows that he can only gain by lowering himself.

143

Instead of consoling our friends over their misfortune, we discuss with them how they could have avoided it.

144

We regret having annoyed others less often than we regret not having annoyed others enough.

145

A failing that we do not want to give up, we like to increase to the utmost, in the hope that others will find something admirable in its extraordinary magnitude, and on this assumption we are so vain about our failings that we perceive them in others only unwillingly.

146

Brawls at which we are onlookers are never fierce enough for us.

147

Men are rational in fighting duels when death or mortal injury is more bearable for them than being held cowards.

148

The brave man is one who is not afraid in the face of pain and death and behaves accordingly.

Courage is highly esteemed, for whoever possesses it can risk everything; rulership over the world and humanity belongs to him, he is independent of all the circumstances of life—he stands *above* them; whereas in contrast the coward can risk nothing, is dependent on the circumstances of life, and stands *beneath* them.

The brave man is morally praiseworthy only when he takes pain and death upon himself for others.

149

Whoever is open and honest going into the struggle of life is like an unarmed man fighting against armed men.

150

Prisoners are no worse than other men: they have only made worse calculations. Accordingly, even their physiognomy usually has nothing evil about it.

151

Whoever has a good reputation tries to maintain it; but whoever has a bad reputation usually doubts the possibility of changing it into a good one and therefore prefers to increase the failing for which he is notorious to the greatest extent. If he cannot gain respect, he can at least create a sensation, which pleases his vanity, while at the same time he fully satisfies his inclination.[12]

152

Seen from without, the actions and events of human life seem to be very diverse and different, but seen from within, they are almost all caused by a very small number of drives, namely, by the drive to survive and get one's living, the sexual drive, and vanity.

153

The failings for which we blame individual persons very often belong to them not as individuals but as members of the species. For example, a certain monarch dismisses and promotes his favorites not according to their merits but according to his whims. Almost everyone would act the same way if he were a ruler. Thus we attribute unjustly to the particular character what is a consequence of particular circumstances and universal human character.

154

We laugh about those who accept our compliments.

155

It was asked how self-respect arose. Somebody answered: From lack of self-knowledge.

156

Anyone who does not make himself liable to the stocks or even the gallows when he behaves quite naturally, belongs among the extraordinary persons.

157

We claim that the opinion of the world is a matter of complete indifference to us, in order to be admired by the world.

158

A philosopher who came back after ten thousand years would probably be astonished not so much by what had altered in the human race as by what had remained unaltered.

159

We take everyone to be bad until they have proved the opposite.

160

If the bad opinion of others were truly a matter of indifference to us, we would not go to so much trouble to convince them of our indifference.

161

The sorrow we feel at the misfortune of our friends is less than the envy aroused by their good fortune.

162

We do not always notice when others are good to us, but we always notice when we are good to others.

163

In our vices we often find aspects of which we are vain.

164

Joy over our own good fortune is seldom as unmixed as joy over the misfortune of our enemies.

165

One admits one's failings in order to bring to mind the virtues bound up with them.

166

We strive for most good qualities only to arouse admiration and envy through them.

167

Men are as Shakespeare depicts them, but out of fear of punishment and disgrace, they act differently in everyday life.

168

The vices of those who take pleasure in their vices become unbearable.

169

Martyrs prefer the feeling of being admired to physical comfort.

170

In times of unrest, when what is dishonorable is neither regarded as dishonorable nor punished, people reveal themselves as they are.

When a state of peace and order returns, they all present themselves as they are not: each person controls and disguises himself as much as is needed to avoid incurring either the legal punishment of his society or the contempt or disapproval of public opinion—which has its origin in a few persons who set the tone.

Accordingly, the more humanitarian practices of one time are to be understood not as an advance of humanitarian feeling but only as a higher degree of self-control and disguise.

This also explains the fact that times of unrest among civilized peoples bear much the same stamp as among uncivilized peoples.

171

Our reason is sometimes strong enough to reach a very virtuous decision but is only seldom capable of carrying it through.

172

One infers from oneself to others, but seldom from others to oneself.

173

Two people are often very tender toward each other, call themselves friends, value their good fortune in being together, cannot separate themselves, and speak with pain of their future separation, when at heart the one curses the presence of the other.

174

In order not to submit to the will of others, we behave even against our inclination and against our interests.

175

We often submit ourselves to suffering to annoy others.

176

The wish to annoy another person can become the motive for suicide.

177

Often we associate with a person not so much out of regard for him as because he has shown regard for us.

178

We condemn the failings of our friends not by how great they actually are, but rather by how much we have to suffer by them. So we condemn their wickedness and extravagant life less than the way they speak so much of themselves or are proud of their superior birth (make themselves important).

179

We often speak well of someone in the hope of being contradicted.

180

One seldom attributes one's own successes to luck, or the successes of others to their merits.

181

When one wants to arouse admiration or envy, one must not let this intention be noticed. For in that case the public, instead of envying our good qualities (which is unpleasant to them), ridicule our intention (which is pleasant to them).

182

We often sacrifice our interest for our friends, since our vanity finds some kind of recompense in that, yet we never sacrifice our vanity itself (our reputation, our popularity, our honor as eminent persons, etc.) to them but rather are much more prepared to sacrifice them to our vanity.

183

We often extol the merits of one person in order to bring to mind the faults of another.

184

Our principles have a great influence on the names we give to the motives of our actions.

185

We engage in friendly public conversation with persons whose social standing is lower than ours only where their and our situations are familiar to everyone.

186

Everyone makes the abilities or good qualities he is proud of possessing into the measure for the worth of everyone else.

187

Men lie to further their interests, but women lie because lying itself gives them pleasure.

188

A youth who gives himself over to vice will, like the fruit infested by a worm, become ripe before his time.

189

Many a person puts on a striking piece of clothing and later convinces himself that the glances directed at him go to prove his fine figure and intelligent physiognomy.

190

Few have such a strong memory that they can keep up the hundredth part of their lies.

191

Parvenus behave badly to their inferiors because they need to emphasize again and again the distinction between themselves and them.

192

We condemn the bad qualities of one person so strongly because we have a mistaken opinion of the good qualities of other people.

193

Every person regards his own deficiencies as the failings of his virtues and usually regards the merits that he concedes to others as the virtues of their failings.

194

That we make ourselves important is always noticed by the public and never by us.

195

People hold nothing against us so badly as their own stupidity.

196

Often we act in a friendly way to make the unfriendliness of others noticeable and to display our own behavior to best advantage by contrast.

197

A good person is one whose gifts a noble person is glad to accept.

198

We love nobody so selflessly that we would not like to be rid of him.

199

It is dangerous to submit oneself or another to hard laws, because if they are not obeyed and other laws are not at hand, one will follow only one's inclinations and passions.

200

It is more rational to resign oneself to the failings of one's surroundings than to want to correct them.

201

Many a person is hard and inconsiderate not out of natural hardness, but because he enjoys the role of a hard and inconsiderate person.

A different person is kind because he enjoys the role of a tender-hearted, considerate, kind person.

202

To many natures, a life without quarrelling and fighting is unbearably boring.

203

The better we know the human heart, the more lenient we are toward its particular expressions.

204

It is easier to refrain from sensual pleasures altogether than to keep them in moderation.

205

We console ourselves over someone's noticing our failing if he displays the same failing himself: from which it is clear that being burdened with a failing is not as painful to us as having a failing that someone else does not have.

206

People have tender feelings at the moment of departure; they feel deep pain at having to part company and regret deeply any previous disagreements. But if some chance event postpones the parting for a short while, they fill in that time with a lively renewal of the disagreement.

207

Our habit of ignoring people who stand lower than us in society occurs not out of arrogance (as the victims usually believe, in order to condemn us all the more strongly) but rather out of fear of being less valued by our equals. If we do not ignore them, it is because we suppose that we cannot get away from them, or because we think our status will not suffer through acquaintance with them, or because we do not want to be taken as arrogant.

In any case, the victims are offended less in their feelings of friendship than in their vanity and act the same way with those who stand lower than themselves.

208

The actings of benevolence and love of one's neighbor on the one hand, and of envy and malicious pleasure on the other, depend no more on us than the actings of our internal organs.

209

We like to cloak our inclinations with the concept of duty.

210

We believe sincerely and firmly everything that we have an interest in believing.

211

It is easier to be friendly to strangers, and even self-sacrificing, than to one's closest relations.

212

We always feel it when someone injures us, but we do not always feel it when we injure others.

213

Whoever demands of his children or friends that they should behave toward him with more kindness is demanding that they pretend to more kindness.

214

The missteps of beautiful women are especially condemned by the ugly, the pride of the aristocracy by the bourgeois, and the satirical scorn of wits by those who lack wit.

215

Our kindness toward formerly rich or respected persons arises from the thankful feeling that we no longer have to suffer from their splendor or from their superiority.

216

Instead of consoling our friends over their misfortunes, we point out that we saw them coming.

217

We minimize someone's merits in order to minimize our own feeling of envy.

218

Luxury of every kind quickly goes to extremes, since everyone keeps wanting to have something that others do not have.

219

The enthusiasm with which we give our friends pieces of advice arises less from concern for them than from the enjoyment of keeping them under instruction.

220

That we are friendly to those who are rejected by everyone else occurs less from benevolence than because we do not want to go with the crowd: we gain more attention when we alone take the opposing side; also, we exercise such friendliness only when our status is high enough not to be endangered by doing so.

221

The best actions often have unsavory inner parts.

On Women, Love, and Marriage

222

It is characteristic of first love that we do not understand how other people before us could have loved, since they had no knowledge of the only object that appears to us worthy of love.

223

Few have loved. With most, a mixture of sensuality and vanity occupies the place of love.

224

Dangers and women are like nettles—not be grasped cautiously.

225

Women need only a little wit to be regarded as witty.

226

Every wife prizes most highly the qualities in men that are lacking in her husband.

227

Every wife is unhappy with her husband and knows another man with whom she would be happy.

228

If, having come to know a noble, intelligent, and deeply sympathetic woman, we finally also achieve an intimate possession of her, we always lose more than we win.

229

Whoever has the wish to be loved by as many people of the other sex as possible—without wanting to seduce, marry, or violate them or to achieve any positive advantage—is a coquette.

This wish is either visible in glances and gestures or invisible, and further, either conscious or unconscious.

Conscious coquetry is usually invisible, and unconscious coquetry usually visible.

When conscious coquetry is visible it offends, whereas unconscious coquetry has something attractive about it.

One subtle kind of visible coquetry is that which seems unconscious and is conscious.

The way in which coquetry expresses itself is thus manifold, and yet its strength is not very different in different persons.

One takes pleasure in coquetry partly because it is pleasant to see people of the other sex at one's feet, but especially because one wants to be envied by persons of the same sex for one's conquests.

230

Girls always attribute the successes of other girls to coquetry.

231

Beautiful women are proud of their conquests, ugly women of their virtue.

232

Women never appear more incomprehensible to us in their taste than when they prefer others to us.

233

Lifelong marriage is a useful but unnatural institution.

234

The degree of married happiness stands in an inverse relation to the amount of shared daily life.

235

In the marriages of our time, no feeling plays such a minor role as love.

236

It is delightful not to seduce a girl who stands on the point of giving herself to us: for our vanity is satisfied by her consent, and we exchange the fleeting enjoyment of love for the pleasant feeling of our high chivalry.

237

In love one makes the other's coldness a reproach in order to conceal one's own coldness.

238

The tactic that wives use in defending their assertions is extremely sensible.

First of all, they express the assertion, perhaps with the addition of a weak argument. When the husband has comprehensively refuted this argument, they express their assertion for a second time in a somewhat more annoying tone, without adding anything to it. The husband, rather surprised at still having made no progress, explains his refutation from as many points of view as possible, but the wife merely repeats her assertion or, when she is sick of the subject, complains of migraine and nervous exhaustion, upon which the Red Cross flag is brought out and any further attack is forbidden by international law.

239

The female sex is by nature no more flirtatious than the male; but whereas the ambition of men can motivate them in various directions, there exists for all the ambitious strivings of women only one direction: conquests.

240

Coquetry is the ambition of the female sex.

241

When a man marries, he has usually already possessed dozens of women; since his fantasy and his desire for variety has ceased to be felt, he stays faithful to his wife from exhaustion.

In contrast, the fantasy of woman is first aroused by married life, and even though she loves her husband more in the first stage of marriage than before, she nevertheless soon becomes tired of him and longs for variety.

242

Normally the unfaithfulness of a young wife arises less out of inclination for her lover than from being tired of her husband.

243

When one can no longer love, one thinks about marriage.

244

Girls are less pained by having no husband than by the thought that people might believe they could not get a husband.

245

However often one may be claim to be right against one's wife, the wife is always in the right.

246

Lovers are never more tender toward each other than when they want to conceal their boredom.

247

One can protect oneself against the unfaithfulness of one's lover only by regarding it in advance as inevitable.

248

An unsuccessful lover is less pained because he must do without the pleasures of love than because another is preferred to him, and a successful lover enjoys being preferred almost more than the pleasures of love.

249

Our love grows with the annoyance of the rejection we have undergone.

250

Vanity is the nurse of love.

Certainly there is a true love that needs no nurse since, like Minerva, it comes into the world already grown.

251

Nearly everyone gets married because they are not known, almost nobody because they are known.

252

Nobody would covet his neighbor's wife if he knew her as well as his neighbor does.

253

Men rule, women tyrannize.

254

Every woman encourages the ambition of her husband, less because he stands out from other men through it as because she stands out from other women through it.

255

The lover wants to possess, the vain person to be desired.

256

The more happiness we promise ourselves on the possession of an object, the more unhappy we become through its possession. Hence, marriages for love are nearly always unhappy, and marriages for money comparatively happy.

257

Toward one's wife, one's subordinates, and one's servants, one must show no distrust. For this suggests to them the possibility of a betrayal; and it seems less bad to them in that the mistrust itself has, as it were, anticipated it.

Moreover, they are faithful just because they do not want to forfeit their reputation for faithfulness; and finally, there is no little satisfaction in outwitting those who mistrustfully watch our every step.

Hence, it is wise to display the greatest trust—and to maintain the greatest mistrust.

258

Before the world, married couples go on affecting happiness for a long time, even though the world is already well-informed about their unhappiness, down to the smallest detail.

259

However often we ourselves may pretend to love, we always believe ourselves to be sincerely loved.

260

Girls always love men who are already loved by others, in order to take the others down a peg.

261

The female sex prefers proud, pretentious, and impudent men to submissive and modest ones: the former challenge women to dominate them; the latter are already dominated, and therefore arouse no more interest.

262

When love finds love in return, it is often extinguished, even before it has tasted any of the pleasures of love: its basis was neither sensuality nor sympathy but rather vanity.

263

One should not marry: for one's grown children will treat one either with forbearance (which is unpleasant) or without forbearance (which is very unpleasant).

In addition, grown children form an alliance with the mother against the father or with the father against the mother.

264

A wife behaves so well toward her friend and so badly toward her husband not because one's personality is more agreeable than the other's, but just because one is her husband and the other her friend.

If they were allowed to change places, her behavior would be reversed accordingly.

265

Rejection increases love, in part because every object we strive for appears more valuable to us when difficulties crowd in between us and it, but especially because the rejected person now wants not just to satisfy his love by possession of the loved object but at the same time to give satisfaction to his injured vanity, perhaps deeply wounded by the preference given to another.

Hence too the fact acknowledged by all, that jealousy makes our love stronger.

266

Instead of "This girl is a coquette" it would be more correct to say "One can see the coquetry of this girl."

267

One wants the woman who is desired by many in order to be preferred over them.

268

The fact that women make the first slip more slowly than men, but then often sink further and faster, rests not on the specifically female character but on the situation. For the honor of a woman is lost once and for all by the first slip; there is no point then in her doing things by half.

269

Women excuse everything in their favorites and condemn everything in those whom they cannot bear.

270

The suitors of our time scrutinize only the packaging of the bride.

271

A beautiful woman often makes those who do not possess her unhappy, and him who does possess her unhappy as well.

272

Those whom one no longer loves one claims never to have loved. Hence the assurance of all women that they have never loved their husbands.

273

The compliments we offer to women are flattering to them as a tribute to their beauty, grace, and wit, although we make them only in order to be taken as gracious and intelligent ourselves.

274

One wants to please those who are pleased by nobody else for the distinction attached to it. Hence, the female sex loves precisely the most pretentious and contemptuous men.

275

Women take it badly when we surprise them before they have prepared their appearance, although the reverse case disposes them very much in our favor.

276

Women want to please every man, with the natural exception of their own husband.

277

Women are often thrilled by a great man but seldom by his achievements.

278

A wife ceases to make reproaches against her children when the husband joins in; instead she turns about and defends the children against the father.

279

With women one does not converse; one only chats.

280

We often strive for the possession of a person or an object only from an awareness that we are in a position to achieve it.

281

One must marry one's bride before one knows her well: for if one knows her well in the first place, one will never marry her.

282

Someone said: At all betrothals I sense a strong feeling of pleasure—malicious pleasure, naturally.

283

Bigamy would be in a certain respect not impractical: for, if the two wives were to alternate continually with each other, each would be on her best behavior with the husband in order to convince him that the other is at fault.

284

If the love with which we strive for the possession of a woman is combined with jealousy, the woman appears to us more amiable, attractive, and beautiful, and generally more desirable in her own right, whereas we in fact desire her possession only because we want to be preferred over others.

285

A happy love may have advantages over an unhappy one, but the unhappy love lasts longer.

286

The female sex has a preference for pretentious men, in part because they are readily seen through and in part because it is satisfying to take their other women down a peg.

287

When a girl we want to possess but not to marry marries another man, we are pained only little. But if she had preferred another lover to us, that would be extraordinarily painful to us; from which it is clear how little love and how much vanity we have.

288

The painful longing for possession of the loved object is a blissful feeling compared with the feeling of disgust after one has possessed.

289

In the cloakrooms of ballrooms women measure one another with hostile glances; they secretly snicker over unfortunate makeup; with undisguised pleasure a friend congratulates another over her successful makeup when she finds it unsuccessful, while a gown is described as "not as pretty as before" when it is uncommonly pretty; also one observes good advice given over small, appropriate alterations of costume, which is followed by novices under the scornful laughter of the experienced; the siege of the mirror; the satisfied expression with which each one departs the mirror; the affected unrest of those who are sure of their dance partners; the affected calm of the fearful; the envious glances of the fading beauties; the trivial things over which the mothers pass the time while they cast sidelong glances comparing their daughters.

290

Women cry where men act.

291

Cynthia loves one of two men. Along comes Lesbia, who has a natural leaning toward the other. Nevertheless, she loves the first one, to whom she is not at all suited; in order to take him away from Cynthia.

292

When it ceases to be in fashion to recount one's conquests, public morality will be improved by that more than by anything else.

293

The best way to gain the good opinion of a woman is often to gain the bad opinion of her husband.

294

Nothing strengthens a woman in her intention as much as the opposition of her husband.

295

One thinks: With this girl I would have been happy—without considering that one thought the same thing of one's wife.

296

Married couples behave well toward each other so little because interest or vanity do not—as in dealings with strangers—encourage the opposite treatment.

297

Since a woman pesters more forcefully and, as it were, comprehensively than a man, and since men do not understand as well as women how to get away from scolding, ridicule and complaining, punishing glances and accusations, the Bible is completely right: he should be your master.[13]

298

The tie that binds betrothed couples as much as married ones is often the fear of scandal.

299

Often we believe we love a person of the other sex and desire her possession, when we want to be desired by her, out of vanity.

300

Our love grows if its object also pleases our friends, since our vanity can now triumph as well.

Our love decreases if its object is disliked by our friends, since our vanity cannot now triumph, and perhaps even suffers.

301

Women are by nature no more envious than men, but since all women are born competitors, they more often have occasion for envy.

302

The faithfulness of our beloved depends on a condition—whether she finds a better lover or not.

303

In love one tends to be betrayer and betrayed at the same time.

304

A wife is not seldom pleased by the mistakes of her husband, since she can now strengthen her authority through reproaches.

305

Women would surrender themselves more quickly if they were not afraid of lowering themselves in the eyes of the seducer himself.

306

Women seldom grant their favors to a timid man. For they feel embarrassed to show more frailty by their behavior before him than he in his timidity has assumed.

In contrast, the bold man seems to hold them inclined to granting their favors, so that by conceding them, they lose nothing further in his eyes. Also, taking possession confidently involuntarily impresses upon them the thought that it must somehow be grounded in a genuinely justified claim, and some courage is generally required to deprive someone of what he claims as his rightful property.

307

A woman who has happened to hear that important women read the prefaces of books as well (according to Jean Paul) will in future read every preface.[14]

Mixed Thoughts

308

So-called good company tends to be bad company to itself, and vice versa.

309

To maintain oneself easily on the surface of the social element, one must not have a greater specific gravity than this element. Otherwise one sinks under, like a stone in water.

310

One pronounces the name of the person introduced more clearly the more distinguished it sounds, and conversely.

311

We emphasize differences in status in relation to persons who stand only slightly beneath us more sharply than in relation to those who stand far beneath us.

312

The person who is always afraid of being a nuisance is the biggest nuisance.

313

A person of whose propriety we have a high opinion does nothing with impropriety.

314

A universally loved person has mediocre virtues and mediocre vices.

315

A company of genteel fools sees the embarrassment with which a scholar moves among them not without satisfaction. Yet they should reflect that it is only their stupidity that makes him so embarrassed.

316

Good manners are an entry pass with which defects of every kind are admitted very readily in society, whereas a person with poor manners, whatever other qualities he may have, is merely tolerated in society.

317

Whoever concerns himself only with the kernel of things runs up against the world where only the shell matters, that is, pretty much everywhere.

318

Only the person who behaves with impudence can commit great lapses in form without being punished.

319

Persons standing beneath us are easily charmed by us: we need only show them a little friendliness.

In contrast, it is difficult to make people standing higher favorable: this requires knowledge of human nature, self-control, and perhaps lack of character.

320

We can find comfort for the fact that we do not please in society in the nature of those who do please there.

321

Whenever we reveal some clumsiness, tactlessness, or ignorance, in no time we find a perspective that completely excuses us. However, if others slip even to the slightest extent, it remains incomprehensible to us why shame does not make them sink into the ground or leave the country.

322

Tactful people who are aware of what wounds others appear better than they are. For they behave tactfully not so much from natural kindliness as because they do not want to be seen as unkind.

Tactless people appear worse than they are. For they quite often wound but do not notice that they are wounding.

323

Important people find social chatter just as difficult as boring people find conversation about important subjects.

324

Anyone who wants to hide a feeling usually displays the opposite to an unnaturally high degree.

325

Whoever does something improper with boldness conveys his apparent or real conviction that it had to be done, at least to some extent, even to the onlooker.

Whoever does something improper with anxiety or embarrassment appears to have the conviction that it did not have to be done, and this is conveyed very strongly to the onlooker.

326

Candor is the privilege of the superior.

327

Someone who lets a good opportunity pass by seldom knows to wait until the next good opportunity.

328

We displease our superiors more when we are too clever than when we are too stupid. One must hit upon just the right mean that pleases them.

329

People would not live together in society if they were without vanity.

330

Most people would perish of boredom if their vanity did not motivate them.

331

Whether the world speaks well or badly of us depends least of all on whether we are actually good or bad.

332

The aristocracy has always borne itself and behaved as demanded by harmony and beauty. So arose the (inherited) aristocratic appearance.

The bourgeois has always borne himself and behaved as demanded by utility and daily work. So arose the (equally inherited) bourgeois appearance.

333

That we scorn the person who places so much weight on good form does not prevent us from also mocking the person who lacks good form.

334

People always think of us differently than we believe.

335

To find out how others speak about us, we need only recall how we speak of them.

336

Everyone is confined within the circle of his inclinations and tastes: they appear to him reasonable and good, since he has them, and the inclinations of others he finds incomprehensible, insane, since he does not have them.

337

Nobody offends against good form as often as the person who is always afraid of offending against it.

338

Those who let nothing please them, and those who let everything please them, get on just as well in the world.

339

Every person has among his good qualities (of mind, of body, or of external possessions) one that he regards as, so to speak, what is most *worth displaying* about his person. He is proud of this, looks for it in everyone else, and depending on whether they happen to have the same quality or not, values or despises them.

340

We appear laughable out of fear of appearing laughable.

341

One must be very common not to be taken as an eccentric.

342

Wanting to make acquaintances everywhere and all the time betrays a lack of nobility, of birth as much as of spirit.

343

In nearly every moral failing we can still find some aspect that is flattering to us and shows our superiority. But intellectual deficiencies subordinate us inescapably to other people. Hence many want to be taken as egoistic, impudent, overbearing, or inconsiderate, but nobody as stupid.

344

Not letting out a secret, when we could make ourselves interesting by passing it on, goes very hard on our vanity.

345

We seldom read about the characteristics of a great man without feeling hurt.

346

The facts that we dream are imaginary, but the feelings that underlie them usually correspond exactly to our actual state of mind.

347

Dreams reveal our character to us.

348

When two people part after their first meeting, each often thinks only of how charmed the other must be by him. Thus, each is mistaken.

349

Intellectual deficiencies often appear as merits of the heart.

350

That we do not envy the person who is stupid and happy is irrational.

351

The opinions of the average person have arisen not out of rational reflection and comparison with other opinions, but out of habit; he takes the customs of his nation or class to be good, since he has followed only them and seen only them followed from childhood onward.

Hence, he does not have his opinions because he takes them to be rational, rather he takes them to be rational because he has them.

352

The wounding of our vanity pains less than the attempt to gain compensation for the injury. For that presupposes that our vanity and its wounding have been observed.

353

We prize our good qualities, talents, virtues, and vices to the extent that we can satisfy our vanity through them.

354

Anyone who has been asked about something he does not know appears far more stupid to himself than to the questioner.

355

It is as easy to despise less gifted people sincerely as it is difficult to value more gifted people sincerely.

356

Our self-admiration is invulnerable.[15]

357

Our own failings please us well, however unpleasant they may be to other people, just as one finds one's own—pleasant-smelling.

358

Our peculiarities we regard as merits, and others regard them as stupidities.

359

We are annoyed when those who are friendly toward us behave in the same way toward others: we want to please them not just as much as, but more than, the others.

360

Being able to speak comfortably with another person is a lesser sign of sympathy than being able to be silent comfortably with that person.

361

Anyone that does not please us we call unsympathetic, but anyone that *we* do not please, we hate.

362

Of our good qualities, we are modest about those that are pleasant in their own right (like health or contentment), but not about those on account of which we are liked, admired, or envied (like beauty, cleverness, and the like, useful for the satisfaction of vanity).

363

We never speak with greater contempt of the opinion of the world than when it does not respect us.

364

Of a great mass of people who support or oppose something, two or three are following their own judgment, the rest their drive to conform.

365

A person who is sympathetic to us we like to call "little"—"little" because then it is clear how unsympathetic everything great is to us.

366

We ward off being despised and denigrated by regarding the despiser as incompetent or the despised qualities as unimportant.

But if the despiser is competent and the despised quality is important to us, we do not admit the facts of the matter.

367

A foreign physiognomy, when we see it often, no longer makes the impression of the typical on us. The individual character, emerging more and more strongly, displaces the character (type) of the species.

368

Sometimes we do not find ourselves good-looking when we step in front of the mirror, but we stay in front of it until we do.

369

Whoever has made a stupid remark and feels it has an irresistible impulse to make still more.

370

Someone made a general observation that embarrassed his two listeners: each of them thought that the other must have applied it to himself.

371

A miser could not bring himself to buy a new wallet, even though his old one had holes out of which he lost his money.

372

When we have not been able to endure the thought that people have this or that opinion of us, and someone tells us in plain words that he has such an opinion, we do not believe him or we forget it in the same moment.

373

Most speakers have only one attentive listener.

374

We find it unbearable that others tell us about their concerns, since we want to tell them about ours.

375

We often wish for the course of events we have prophesied, even when it is harmful to us.

376

In debates nearly everyone wants less to be instructed and enlightened than to be in the right. Hence, their excitement even over matters that are quite without personal interest. And based on this is the fact that they make the strongest objections precisely against the wisest and soundest arguments instead of accepting them. And if the opponent is finally shown to be in the right, they do not feel pleasure over the knowledge gained but only the shameful feeling of having been wrong.

377

Often we defend our opinion less because we think it is right than because we have said that we think it is right.

378

When we have assigned the character of a person to some category or other, such as an arsonist, we want him to act accordingly from then on.

379

We are always annoyed when an apparently senseless piece of behavior that we regarded as ridiculous turns out to be rational once its motives have emerged.

380

It is more rational to concede to those who are wrong that they are right than to wish to convince them that they are wrong.

381

We act according to principles that we have publicly proclaimed, in order not to appear inconsistent.

382

In our blameworthy behavior, we often act against our inclination, in order not to concede to others that they were right when they blamed that behavior.

383

Status is gained not by good qualities, but by cleverness, high birth, and riches. Hence, we certainly respect good qualities, but envy the clever, eminent, and rich.

384

Irreconcilable hatred is born of envy.

385

The wish to say something very clever usually leads one to say something very stupid.[16]

386

Usually another person finds it precisely as boring to listen to us as we find it interesting.

387

It is wise to admit one's failings to oneself and to hide them from others.

388

Embarrassment is a difficult emotion, for the workings of reason, which are of some use at least with all other emotions, here cause more damage.

389

Our embarrassment is usually unnecessary, since the other person is concerned not with the impression we are making on him, but with the impression he is making on us.

390

Being embarrassed suits the female sex, but not the male.

391

One laughs over one's clumsiness so that others will not laugh over it.

392

Important people are often embarrassed; for they feel that they are different from the rest and are now afraid of appearing laughable to them.

This holds, however, only for theoretical natures, which are distinct in kind from the rest; people distinguished by practical cleverness are not embarrassed, for they have the same qualities that others have to a higher degree.

393

In a state of embarrassment one wishes to hide one's face, for example, with the hand, since that is where embarrassment is displayed. So that this intention is not observed, one does something with one's face, and indeed involuntarily does (as a result of associated habit) precisely whatever it is that one is accustomed to do with one's face. Thus, people who are used to rubbing their sore eyes also rub their eyes in the state of embarrassment, and so on.

394

Genius, rank, or riches do not protect one from embarrassment as securely as a very high degree of stupidity: for its possessor is far removed from any fear of making a bad impression.

395

Our behavior is always without embarrassment when we are preoccupied with some great concern, for then the lesser concern for not making a bad impression is subordinated.

396

It has been claimed that the enjoyment the vain person finds in being admired is based on the fact that admiration makes him think of the possession and the worth of the qualities admired. But if admiration is only a passing factor (as it were, only a means to an end) and in the end what is enjoyed is the worth of the quality admired in its own right, then nobody should be judged as vain: for the person who is vain is precisely the one who is pleased by possession of a good quality because he can achieve admiration by means of that quality (so that the good quality is the means, and admiration is the end).

397

We find it senseless when someone makes talents or possessions we do not have a measure of human worth.

398

Whoever has merits, is aware of them, and expresses this awareness in his behavior is proud.

Whoever has merits and is aware of them but does not express this awareness in his behavior is modest.

Whoever has no merits but thinks he has them is presumptuous.

Whoever has merits but believes he does not have them is faint-hearted.

Whoever despises all classes, with the exception of his own, is arrogant.

Whoever hates all those of a different opinion is fanatical.

Fanaticism is an arrogance of thought, and arrogance a fanaticism of class. But whereas the fanatic would like to kill all those of a different opinion, the arrogant person would find himself in difficulty without people to be submissive.

Whoever displays a feeling he does not have is dissimulating.

Whoever does not display a feeling that he has is self-controlled.

Women are self-controlled, men more often dissimulate.

It is easier to dissimulate than to be self-controlled.

Dissimulation is blameworthy only when it is used to injure another.

399

The French have too little reason and the Germans too much.

400

As soon as we have an interest in holding a particular opinion to be right—whether it is because we have already asserted it, or because being convinced of its incorrectness would deliver us over to the tormenting state of doubt, or to some other uncomfortable or unhappy mood—we hold it to be right.

If this interest happens to disappear, so too our opinion eventually gives way to another; and if it is in our interest to believe the opposite of our earlier view, we are no less firmly convinced of this new opinion than we were of the old one.

On Religious Things

401

Belief and disbelief are not moral qualities, but only opinions.

402

Should we be condemned by God to the eternal torments of hell because our God-given intelligence finds divine revelation obscure and incredible?

403

The orthodox hate the free spirits because they are afraid of being regarded as stupid by them.

404

Whoever is given a ministry by God is also given the political and religious opinions of his ministry.

405

We are given religious instruction at the same age that we have childhood diseases.

406

The state concerns itself only with the utility, not with the truth, of religion; philosophy, in contrast, is concerned only with its truth and not with its utility.

407

When the preacher says "Amen" from the pulpit, the thoughts of every listener return to the church.

408

Ministers of different denominations are at odds less on account of their different views than on account of their shared views.

409

Religious faith often arises not from the simplicity of the heart, but from the simplicity of the head.

410

An orthodox theologian who is torn away from his career by external circumstances seldom remains orthodox.

411

Fear is the mother of belief, and habit is its nurse.

412

The character of ministers appears blacker than the character of other people because it stands out from a lighter background.

413

Conscious hypocrites are rarer than one may think, since they presuppose an unusual energy.

The mass of the ministry consists of unconscious hypocrites, that is, of those who dimly sense that they could not admit their unbelief to themselves without either being hypocrites in the genuine sense or having to resign from their position.

Therefore they do not allow any serious doubt to emerge, but rather thrust the problem aside and think of something else.

Even the other believers feel instinctively that they would lose every fixed support for their ideas and hopes by unbelief.

Hence, self-interest and the longing for happiness are the principal supports for belief in the truth of religion.

It is similar in other things: everything of which clear knowledge would be unpleasant to us, we do not admit to ourselves. So the person in love imagines not being in love, the despised person not being despised, the indifferent person being enthusiastic, and so on.

414

The tears of the listeners are the triumph of the preacher.

415

If our happiness gives us an interest in belief in immortality, we should be mistrustful of the objective truth of this belief.

416

We would not take ourselves to be immortal if the opposite conviction were comfortable.

417

Whether we do something or leave it undone depends on the sensations and thoughts that are present in the moment of our action. They motivate the action necessarily, just as they are themselves motivated by our inborn nature and the influences that have operated on us from birth until the moment of the action. Consequently, all acts of will are necessary acts.

418

If the penitent were to express himself precisely, he would not say, "Oh, that I had left that deed undone," but rather, "Oh, that the sensations and thoughts which gave rise to that deed had not been there!"

419

Ministers support religion because religion supports them.

420

Only a small number of ministers concern themselves any longer with the content of religion, as compared with its salary, or with the judgment of God, as compared with that of the church assembly.

421

Faith is needed (an ugly girl said to me) at times to protect us from despair, such as, over being ugly.

422

Ministers love the appearance of religion from love for their own appearance.

423

When a court is pious, many hold it to be in bad taste not to be pious.

424

Ministers are expected to have a certain feeling at a certain time in a certain place: they must be hypocrites.

425

Actors and preachers have in common, among other things, that one sees their profession in them: their faces, having been so often the place where an unnatural, artificial feeling is displayed, acquires with the passing of time the expression of the unnatural, artificial, and distorted.

On Happiness and Unhappiness

426

The worst thing that can happen to someone who enjoys reflecting on life is that he should find the time to do so.

427

Nobody loves life out of reason.

428

The head destroys our illusions, but the heart always rebuilds them.

429

Even the smallest care is accompanied by the illusion that we would be happy once it were set aside.

430

People commonly bear a small misfortune worse than a great one, since they surrender themselves to it fully; whereas they do not fully surrender themselves to the great misfortune, since they instinctively feel they would be crushed by it, and so seek the comfort that they find in almost any idea.

431

Good fortune had transported me to the outer garden of paradise. As I strolled about there in delight, I came suddenly to a door. "Aha," I thought, "this is the entrance to paradise!" I opened it and stepped across its threshold, whereupon the door fell shut behind me with a crash. Curious, I glanced around me and saw with surprise and horror—that I had stepped through the exit.

432

If someone's pessimistic philosophy of life is abstracted from individual experiences that he himself has had, he will be simultaneously melancholy, depressed, and embittered in his heart. Yet whoever is made aware of human unhappiness through philosophy will not necessarily feel melancholy through this theoretical experience. For a hundred sorrows that we see in others make us, by and large, not as melancholy as one that affects ourselves. And if the observer publishes his findings, then his joy over every new observation, however sad it may be, is greater than the pain he feels as a benevolent person. Hence, someone who depicts human beings as unhappy can be himself a relatively cheerful person.

433

Our happiness depends more on our temperament than on the constitution of our heart.

434

Good people are not necessarily happy, and bad people are not necessarily unhappy.

435

Every person gathers ideas from all people and things, seeing himself in the center of the world. Now the thought that the activity of the world that is mirrored in his head will still go on without him and after his death is, in a way, ungraspable. He has the feeling that the whole world must perish along with him, or at least that the memory of him must be evoked in other people continually and on every occasion.

436

When the envious person has discovered a fault in the envied object, he feels relieved but not yet satisfied; rather, he uses the single fault as a clue to find still more, until the faults finally outweigh the merits in number and importance. Now he is satisfied and passes triumphantly from the unpleasant feeling of envy to one of contempt.

437

Nearly everyone has a favorite worry which, as long as other cares are present in his mind, waits outside the doors of the mind: it takes over the periods of interregnum.

438

Many a person is called a favorite child of happiness, when in fact he is only a favorite dog of happiness.

439

Where passions and their illusions are concerned, the experience of others is of no use to us, and our own of almost no use.

440

Those who are the most envied are the least enviable.

441

Our hopes make us happy as long as they are not fulfilled.

442

It is risky to achieve the satisfaction of one's vanity through great efforts, for example, by building palaces. For often a jest that comes to our ears, even a scornful glance that strikes us at the right moment, is enough to poison the satisfaction entirely for us.

443

We are unhappy because we are not in possession of the object we strive for—that is bearable.

We are unhappy because the possession of the object we strive for does not make us happy—that is unbearable.

444

The assumption that we would be happy in different circumstances is always the worst element of our present circumstances.

445

The number of envied persons is greater than the number of enviable persons.

446

Who would not be fearful of the future if he accepted that it would be like the past?

447

If someone usually full of cares is free of cares for a moment, he is restless until he has discovered a new cause for cares.

448

We always know how to find a consoling aspect in our unhappiness, and we are not consoled for the happiness of others until we have uncovered its bad aspect.

449

Upon the occurrence of every misfortune we complain that we did not realize our happiness before. But that we were happy earlier is just as much an illusion as the hope for a future happiness.

450

The envious person is often mistaken in two respects: insofar as he believes that the envied advantage makes its possessor happy; and insofar as he believes that the envied advantage would make him happy.[17]

451

The person who feels unhappy in the midst of status, health, riches, and beauty is more to be pitied than the person who is made unhappy by lacking those advantages, insofar as he can no longer hope.

452

With every misfortune, whether it is an actual injury or an embarrassment, we are especially annoyed by the superiority in power, appearance, riches, fame, or inherited talent that we must now recognize in others. With the thought that they have lost those advantages, that is, do not possess them, we are accordingly freed of the greatest and most severe part of our pain. On this rests the *socios habuisse malorum*.[18]

453

In youth, we always believe that possession of the prize we are directly striving for will make us happy forever. Whoever has completely overcome this error is a person very much to be pitied.

454

Many people would never find pleasure in nature if they had not heard that nature is beautiful.

455

Tourists often feel a certain discomfort when they come to a beautiful view: they feel that they must affect enthusiasm, to themselves or others.

456

The pleasure of almost all tourists in the mountains is based less on enjoyment of nature than on the overcoming of difficulties.

457

One kind of tourist adopts a particular goal every morning, in fact one as far away as possible in relation to their strength. On the way to it, they are not enjoying themselves and, on arriving at the goal, they are too dull and too concerned with plans for the following day to be able to enjoy anything.

Other tourists want to enjoy themselves continually, and not just upon the overcoming of difficulties: on principle, they find it hard work to climb even the smallest hill, and as a result get to see almost no views. Also, they like to observe one another: Are you really enjoying yourself, is the landscape making an impression on you? In this way they destroy the enjoyment or, since they still want to enjoy themselves, manage a sentimental, artificial semi-enjoyment.

Both classes of people live and study precisely in the way that they travel.

458

Tourists in the mountains are usually interested in nothing so much as the heights and the names of mountains.

459

We are never more delighted by nature than when our delight has a public.

460

People are often thrilled by objects of nature or art in order to be able to recount later how thrilled they were.

461

Nature takes away from its favorite, the genius, his cares. The rest of humanity can enjoy nature only when they enter into it free from cares.

462

In the place of every care that is eliminated grow new cares, like Hydra heads; yet we always think we will become happy after eliminating the previous care.

463

It is rational to satisfy our vanity at the cost of our inclination in the cases where frustration is less unpleasant to us than wounded or unsatisfied vanity, for example, when we would rather be bored with higher-placed persons than amuse ourselves with those standing lower.

464

Whoever has arrived at the conviction that no possession of advantages will make him happy must cease to strive, to be active, at all. This inactivity (boredom) arising from disgust at all activity is the real motive for suicide.

465

The thought that we could be happy in different circumstances is painful; the thought that we could not be happy in any circumstances is annihilating.

466

No feeling is so much a punishment in its own right as envy.

467

The decision to kill oneself arises from an excess of rationality.

468

That we were happy as children is an optical illusion; small cares make the child just as unhappy as great cares make adults.

469

When our hopes have gained fulfillment, we are commonly more unsatisfied than before, after the first rush of joy. For in the place of hope there is now the feeling of emptiness, and this does not disappear until the fulfilled wish is replaced by another one.

470

We admit uncomfortable feelings to our minds only in disguise.

471

In spite of all experience, we do not learn that good and bad moods pass over. Hence, we fail to benefit from the former and suffer twice as badly from the latter.

472

In order to dispel our light-hearted mood, we sometimes conjure up the saddest images. But the subjective mood can prevail so much over the objective impression that the very thoughts that make us melancholy at other times are now not taken seriously.

473

What we regard as the reason for our bad humor is commonly painful in consequence of our bad humor.

474

The resolution of Regulus is no doubt praiseworthy to the highest degree, but perhaps not satisfactory.[19] For it was his *resolution* that gave rise to the dilemma: either living in Rome and feeling the bite of conscience, or being put to death in Carthage—this at any rate being compensated for to a certain degree by the feeling of the fulfillment of duty.

A laxer and less conscientious person would have lived comfortably in Rome—a situation perhaps to be preferred to the death-pains of the martyr of conscience, even if they are supplemented by the feeling of the fulfillment of duty.

475

A melancholy person would not feel as good in heaven as a cheerful person would in hell.

Essay on Vanity

For two reasons, it is not a matter of indifference to people whether others take them to be good or bad, clever or stupid, good-looking or ugly, poor or rich, friendly or unfriendly: (1) because they are self-interested, and so hope for advantages from a good opinion and are afraid of disadvantages from a bad opinion; or (2) because they are vain, so that a good opinion (i.e., being pleasing, admired, envied) is itself pleasant and a bad opinion (i.e., being mistrusted, ridiculed, disparaged, despised) is itself unpleasant.

Positive vanity can be divided into vanity in a narrower sense and ambition.

It is characteristic of the person who is vain in the narrower sense that he is satisfied with the amount of admiration and envy he enjoys at present, whereas the ambitious person is not satisfied with this: the latter wants to achieve more admiration—if possible, to be more admired and envied than anyone else.

This is why ambition cannot refer to pleasing, since the qualities by which we please are not acquired.

The negative side of vanity (on account of which it is painful to be disparaged and despised) is called in everyday language the feeling of honor.

The existence of vanity is a problem. Why pleasing and being admired should be pleasant in their own right, and being disparaged and despised should be painful in their own right, is unclear.

Let us suppose that the first human beings who lived together in herd fashion were without vanity; that is, being admired or despised, even pleasing or displeasing, were indifferent to them. Then they would still sometimes have wanted to be pleasing, for example, to the woman of their choice (for even at the first stage of civilization, women do not accept every individual man, but like the females of almost all other animals make a choice, as Darwin has sufficiently proven). If rejected, they felt not their disparagement and the preference given to others but only deprivation of the enjoyment of love. Nevertheless they would sometimes have wished that their achievements, for example, the weapons they had made, would be admired, especially when they wanted to exchange these for other objects.

Now, if their person or achievements were admired in cases where they could not foresee an immediate advantage, then, taught by experience how advantageous being admired could sometimes be, they might quite well have felt admiration as pleasant and its opposite as unpleasant. Thus, the first step on the way to vanity was taken. For if we assume that when admired or despised they foresaw the immediate consequences more often, then they would gradually have became used to foreseeing the general consequences and to feeling that all pleasing and being admired were pleasant in their own right, and all disparagement and being despised painful in their own right.

In addition, if pleasing and being admired were pleasant to them in the cases in which they expected an advantage from them, they would become accustomed through associated habit to feel them as more or less pleasant even in the cases in which they expected no advantage.

The instinct or drive thus achieved is then passed on to the descendants and is reinforced by continual activity over many generations.

In the end, vanity must have become extraordinarily strong through natural selection, since in the struggle for existence the race that survived was the one that contained the greatest number of vain people. Since the vain wanted admiration, and admiration is especially given to the courageous, vain men would raise their courage higher than those who were less vain or not vain at all. In addition, ambition encourages the invention of useful arts and sciences; and the feeling of honor forbids being unusually cowardly, dishonest or lazy, or committing crimes which, being harmful to the race, bring on themselves punishment and disgrace.

Hence, as we have said, the race proceeding from the vainest men will survive.

❧

Now, if being admired is pleasant, then almost everything by which we recognize that we are admired will give pleasure: above all envy, insofar as it is envy of our pleasing and being admired, or envy of those of our good qualities by which we please and are admired.*

This is one of the reasons why vanity is condemned: it gives us the occasion to enjoy others' envy of us, or sometimes to feel envy and jealousy ourselves.

A further reason is its irrationality: since we do not always please when we

---

* Every person finds himself as it were in competition with others: he wants to please more, to be admired more, to be envied more than them; and malicious pleasure is based on the feeling that others are kept behind us, that is, have no advantages over us.

want to please, and in any case, the pleasure in pleasing is much less than the pain suffered in displeasing; since furthermore almost nobody is so famous, good-looking, or rich that he does not more often feel envy than arouse envy; and also since the feeling of envy is more painful than the provoking of envy is pleasant; and since the person who enjoys admiration and envy in the greatest measure very soon loses this enjoyment through habit—so vanity brings us much sorrow and little joy. We would be happier without vanity. Nevertheless we cannot do anything about it. For it is now an inborn and powerful drive, so that we involuntarily take pleasure in pleasing and pain in displeasing. To wipe out this joy and this pain for every occasion is not possible, and the attempt to do so would be more painful than to feel them without opposition.

A third reason, in conclusion, why the vain person is blamed is his lack of serious and objective commitment: for whereas the genius, as such, concerns himself only with subjects, and indeed, is concerned with them for their own sake, the vain person concerns himself only with striving to please and be admired and is not concerned with subjects in general, or is concerned only insofar as he can please and achieve admiration through a knowledge of them.

Nobody admits his vanity (although everyone is *very* vain), in part because it is forbidden for the reasons of immorality, irrationality, and lack of objectivity already mentioned, and in part because we do not want to appear dependent on the opinion of others but would rather present ourselves as if their opinion were indifferent to us, indeed, as if we despised it.

The ambitious person is also blamed for his irrationality. For he is unsatisfied, and however hard he may labor, however much fame, wealth, and reputation he may achieve, the unsatisfied state remains, and with it the hard labor.

On the other hand, one must consider that the labor of the ambitious person, however hard it may be, is a far lesser pain than the boredom most people would fall into if they were without ambition.

In addition, the ambitious person, like the vain one, is blamed for his bad goal, that of arousing as much admiration and envy as possible—yet not blamed as strongly as the vain person, for the following reason. With the vain person, the aim results immediately: he wants to be admired now. With the ambitious person the aim stays at first in the background: what appears immediately is only the highest straining and labor of mental forces, which tends to be useful to the community.

Here the means justify the end, so to speak.

In general the ambitious person is hard-working, and the vain person lazy.

One likes to say one is ambitious in order to claim that one has the will and the capacity to excel over others.

One also often claims to be without ambition in order to indicate that one willingly concerns oneself with objects for the sake of the objects, or works for people for their own sake.

Having a sense of honor is irrational in the same way, since it gives rise almost exclusively to feelings of displeasure—especially when we are disparaged or despised. Also, the feeling of honor creates this dilemma: either we follow our inclination, and then often bring upon ourselves the disparagement of the world; or else we conform to the opinion of the world. In that case, we must often act against our inclination.

Whether we choose being ruled by and protecting the sense of honor or following inclinations and injuring the sense of honor depends on character and circumstances. In either case, we suffer because we have the sense of honor.

The sense of honor gives pleasure only when we can restore our injured honor as good, clever, brave, good-looking, tactful people—which is seldom or never the case.

The sense of honor is not morally blameworthy. For in having the feeling of honor, we do not want to arouse either admiration or envy, we only fear being disparaged and despised; we do not want to be either wiser or better, but merely to be taken as no more stupid and bad than others.

But the sense of honor is not really morally praiseworthy either; for it contains no unegoistic, selfless elements. Whoever is, for example, brave in order not to be regarded as cowardly, is acting for himself, given his motive, not acting for others.

Nevertheless the sense of honor is always taken as praiseworthy on account of its extraordinary usefulness. One must reflect that society, in contrast with the state of nature, is an unnatural condition. The natural wish of every individual to satisfy his desires at the cost of everyone else is artificially kept in bounds by the fear of punishment and disgrace. But the fear of disgrace is greater than the fear of punishment; and only disgrace pains one continually, often throughout one's whole life. Hence, it remains at least doubtful whether, if the fear of shame did not exist, even a draconian set of laws could restrain individuals from continual offences against others. At any rate, the maintenance of social peace and order is made easier to a very high degree by the existence of the sense of honor.*

In addition, the sense of honor is useful in many aspects of private life, in particular within education.

It is based on this that, as we have said, the feeling of honor is always treated as a virtue, despite its not at all selfless nature and despite its irrationality.

---

* Since the duel is one of the liveliest manifestations of the sense of honor, it is actually encouraged by every government.

NOTES

1. From Gobineau's *Essai sur l'inégalité des races humaines*, as cited by Schopenhauer in *Parerga and Paralipomena*, 2:214. It is derived from a line in Molière's *Tartuffe*, act 5, scene 6: "L'homme est, je vous l'avoue, un méchant animal."

2. Vauvenargues, *Réflexions et maximes*, no. 299, *Oeuvres complètes*, 2:433.

3. "The unities of Aristotle": Aristotle, *Poetics*, chaps. 7–8, *Basic Works* 1462–63.

4. The fable of the wren is attributed to Aesop by Plutarch in his *Moralia*, 10:201.

5. Vauvenargues, *Réflexions et maximes*, no. 52, *Oeuvres complètes*, 2:407.

6. "To him who has shall be given": Matt. 25:29.

7. "Pleasant it is, when over a great sea the winds trouble the waters, to gaze from shore upon another's great tribulation: not because any man's troubles are a delectable joy, but because to perceive what ills you are free from yourself is pleasant." Lucretius, *De rerum natura*, book 4, lines 1–4. These lines are quoted by Schopenhauer in *The World as Will and Representation*, sect. 58, vol. 1, p. 320.

8. A German proverb: "Wer den Schaden hat, braucht für den Spott nicht zu sorgen."

9. Schopenhauer writes, "On the other hand, the suffering caused by the arbitrary action of another has, in addition to the pain or damage itself, something quite peculiar and bitter, namely, the consciousness of the other man's superiority, whether through force or cunning, and of our own impotence. If possible, the damage inflicted is made good by reparation, but that additional bitterness, namely, the thought: 'I have to put up with this from you', which often causes more pain than does the injury itself, can be neutralised only by revenge. Thus by inflicting injury, either by force or cunning, on the man who has injured us, we show our superiority and thereby annul evidence of his. This gives our feelings the satisfaction for which they thirsted. Accordingly, there will be a great thirst for revenge where there is much pride or vanity." *Parerga and Paralipomena*, 2:589.

10. "He who humbles himself shall be exalted": Matt. 23:12; Luke 14:11, 18:14. Cf. Nietzsche's *Human, All-Too-Human*, sect. 87: "Luke 18:14 improved.—He who humbles himself wants to be exalted."

11. "Love those that hate you": Matt. 5:44, Luke 6:27.

12. "If he cannot gain respect [*Ansehen*], he can at least create a sensation [*Aussehen*]" is a play on words.

13. See Eph. 5:22–23; Col. 3:18; Titus 2:5; 1 Pet. 3:1, 3:5.

14. "Jean Paul" is the German author Johann Paul Friedrich Richter (1763–1825).

15. "Our self-admiration [*Selbstbewunderung*] is invulnerable [*unverwundbar*]" is another play on words.

16. Cf. La Rochefoucauld, *Maxims,* no. 199: "Desire to appear clever often prevents our becoming so."

17. Cf. ibid., no. 543: "Before strongly desiring anything we should look carefully into the happiness of its present owner."

18. *Socios habuisse malorum:* "having companions in misfortune." Schopenhauer writes, "Even when actual evils have befallen us, the most effective consolation, although flowing from the same source as envy, is afforded by the thought of greater sufferings than ours and then by association with those who are in the same situation, the *socii malorum.*" *Parerga and Paralipomena,* 1:431.

19. The Roman general Regulus was captured by the Carthaginians, who allowed him to go to Rome for peace negotiations on condition that he agree to return to them. When no settlement was reached, Regulus went back to face death rather than break his word.

PART 2

The Origin of the Moral Sensations

CONTENTS

PREFACE

The point of view of this essay is a purely theoretical one. Just as the geologist begins by seeking out and describing different formations and then inquires into the causes from which they have arisen, so too the author has begun by taking up moral phenomena from experience, and has then gone into the history of their beginning, as far as his abilities allowed.

No doubt what he gives is not so much a systematic work as a collection of individual observations. If he were blamed for that he would, making a virtue of necessity, defend himself in the following manner. Every genuine thinker is an occasional thinker: ideas come only on occasion, and hence not about every aspect of a subject. Anyone who wants to treat a subject exhaustively must therefore often think ad hoc, and often force his thoughts. There are gaps in this essay, but gaps are better than stopgaps.

INTRODUCTION

Moral philosophy is concerned with human actions. At the outset it states that certain actions are felt as good, others as bad; that bad actions often give rise to remorse; that on account of the so-called sense of justice we demand punishment for bad actions.

These moral phenomena are often considered to be something supersensible—the voice of God, as the theologians put it. In his essay *Religion within the Limits of Reason Alone,* Kant denied decisively the communication between this world and the other, which the church calls revelation. He had also demonstrated in his *Critique of Pure Reason* that no knowledge at all of the transcendent is possible, because our power of knowledge is valid only within space and time. Despite all this, even Kant saw in moral consciousness something transcendent, to a certain extent a revelation from the transcendent world. Admittedly, before the theory of evolution appeared, many of these phenomena could not be explained by immanent causes, and a transcendent explanation is certainly far more satisfying than—none at all. Yet today, since Lamarck and Darwin have written, moral phenomena can be traced back to natural causes just as much as physical phenomena: moral man stands no closer to the intelligible world than physical man.

This natural explanation rests essentially on the following proposition: The higher animals have developed by natural selection from lower ones, for instance, human beings from the apes.

I do not go into the reasons for this proposition. For I consider it to be proven by the writings of Darwin, and in part already by those of Lamarck. Anyone who has a different opinion may as well leave the present work unread: since he denies the premises, he cannot agree with the conclusions.

CHAPTER 1

The Origin of the Concepts "Good" and "Evil"

Every person combines two drives within himself, namely, the egoistic drive and the non-egoistic drive.

Through the egoistic drive he strives for his own welfare, above all his own preservation, the satisfaction of his sexual instinct, and the satisfaction of his vanity.

The satisfaction of each of these particular forms of the egoistic instinct can possibly do harm to the welfare of other people; for instance, to preserve one's own life, one will perhaps destroy someone else's; to satisfy one's sexual instinct, one will perhaps destroy a woman's happiness, or kill one's rival. Vanity finally inspires the desire to please and be admired. Anyone who has this desire—and everyone does—will however hate those who please and are admired more than himself. He will therefore try to bring them down, to eliminate them, and if this succeeds he will feel malicious pleasure [*Schadenfreude*]. Vanity can lead to injuring others in other ways as well: for instance, in order to be admired for one's wealth, one may perhaps acquire the property of others in an unjust fashion.

On account of the non-egoistic drive, a man makes the welfare of others the final end of his actions, whether he seeks their welfare for their own sake or refrains from harming them for their own sake.

The person who acts in a non-egoistic way is also called compassionate, benevolent, and charitable.

The fact that the egoistic actions just described are not only possible but occur all the time clearly indicates that the non-egoistic instinct is weak. Some philosophers, Helvétius in particular, even claim that non-egoistic sensations or actions are not present at all in human nature, and that what seems to be non-egoistic is only a disguised form of the egoistic drive. They say: anyone who sees other people suffer cannot help imagining their pain. The idea of this pain produces a sensation of displeasure, and this is called compassion.

This sort of compassion is certainly often found, but it is not the only kind. Sometimes we feel pain not only because we imagine the sufferings of another person but rather because just the fact of his suffering makes us suffer; our feeling is non-egoistic. For example, a mother who sees her child suffering does not feel the pain because she imagines the child's suffering—in that case, the person of the child would be indifferent to her—rather, it is just the fact that the child suffers that pains her. This non-egoistic compassion does not appear solely in parental love but in many other cases as well. Further, if anyone who feels compassion in the first sense helps those for whom he feels compassion, this does without doubt occur out of egoism, that is, in order to free himself from the mental picture of a pain. On the other hand, if someone who feels compassion in the second (non-egoistic) sense helps the person for whom he feels compassion, that occurs in order to relieve the other's suffering; he helps for the other's sake and not for his own—for example, the mother acts solely to free the child from its pain, and thus for the child's sake, not for her own. That such non-egoistic actions actually occur is shown by observation, first and foremost by self-observation. Moreover, since non-egoistic compassion (pain over the suffering of others) exists, non-egoistic actions must also exist. For if it is possible to feel pain because someone else is suffering, it must be equally possible to act because another person is suffering. In this case, the sensation is to behavior as the thought is to the act.

Certainly, non-egoistic actions are also accompanied by feelings of pleasure. In fact, when we help a suffering person for his own sake, what disappears at the same time as his suffering is our painful mental picture of his suffering, and our pain over the fact that he is suffering; and there arises in us the pleasant feeling of having performed a good deed (see what follows)—if we had failed to perform the good deed, we would perhaps later have felt remorse. But these feelings of pleasure that arise on the occasion of a helpful action, or fear of the unpleasant feeling of remorse, are nevertheless not the motivation of non-egoistic actions. Helvétius is wrong when he generalizes: "We relieve the unfortunate, 1. To avoid the bodily pain of seeing them suffer. 2. To enjoy an example of gratitude, which produces in us at least a confused hope of distant utility. 3. To exhibit an act of power, whose exercise is always agreeable to us, because it recalls to the mind the images of pleasure attached to that power."[1]

Not all helpful acts have such motivations.

Sympathetic pleasure [*Mitfreude*] admits of a similar distinction. First of all, just as the suffering of others does not always arouse compassion, but often malicious pleasure instead, so too the happiness of others does not always arouse sympathetic pleasure, but more often envy. Even when it does arouse pleasure, this may be of two sorts: either the mental picture of a happy state, to which we are involuntarily stimulated by the presence of this state in others, makes us happy; or the fact that others are happy makes us happy. This latter non-egoistic sympathetic pleasure is often called benevolence.

Moreover, anyone who refrains from harming others will most of the time be acting out of egoism, for example, out of fear of punishment; yet we often impose limits on our drives and desires for the sake of others themselves, out of compassion and benevolence.

Thus, a non-egoistic interest in the fate of others, whether one calls it compassion, benevolence or love of one's neighbor, does exist.

But how are non-egoistic actions possible? How does a person come to care for others often as much as for himself?

This question was not even raised by Hutcheson, even though he strongly defends the existence of non-egoistic actions. He merely says that we act in that way because of an innate feeling.[2] But now the question arises again of where this innate feeling comes from. Hume too says only, "From the original frame of our temper, we feel a desire of another's happiness or good," without further explaining the existence of this benevolence.[3] Schopenhauer, in contrast, explains the possibility of selfless actions, and does so in the following way:

Space is, according to Kant, a form of perception a priori; our apparatus of knowledge is organized in such a way that we represent things as spatial; but in itself, independently of the representation of a representing subject, space does not belong to things. So what are things in themselves, stripped of the spatial form in which they appear to the representing subject? That remains hidden from us, because we know things only in the form of space and cannot know what is nonspatial.

On the other hand, let us reflect: the essence of every being, as it presents itself empirically, is the will to live. The bodily organization of man, as well as his drives and his intellectual faculties (understanding and reason) serve this end alone and stand in the service of his will to live. In the same way, the organization of all other beings, of plants and animals, is dedicated to their will to live. Indeed, even the properties of matter, such as gravity, must be considered by analogy with other beings as if the will to live were "objectified" in them. Copernicus says, "I believe that gravity is only a natural striving (*appetentia*) which the divinity has implanted in the parts so that they will unite in one whole and in this way survive undamaged." (See Schopenhauer, "On the Will in Nature."[4]) The will is the soul of every thing. Human beings, animals, plants, and matter are only different spatial forms of appearance of the same fundamental force.

If one were, however, to regard the will to live as a thing in itself, and human beings, animals, etc., as spatial appearances of this thing in itself, that would contradict the principle that the thing in itself cannot be known. Yet the fact that, I repeat, human beings, animals, etc., only represent spatially in various ways one and the same fundamental force, namely, the will, forces us to consider the world of appearance *as if* the will to live as a thing in itself were its basis. In Kant's language, which Schopenhauer admittedly does not use in this case, one could say: The will is not a constitutive but a regulative principle.

Nevertheless, if we consider the will to live as a thing in itself, we must regard it as nonspatial and therefore not as something multiple or composite, but as a unity. To the representing subject, there certainly appear as many single wills as there exist single things. But the will spun out in this way is still only a phenomenon: since we have representations only in the form of space, we can represent even the will only spatially, that is to say, spun out and divided into individuals. In itself it is just one, as all things, though they present themselves to the subject of knowledge as many objectifications of the will, are in themselves—just one.

Now, in compassion, when a person cares for others as for himself, the semblance as if things were fundamentally divided into individuals disappears momentarily. The oneness of things breaks through, the compassionate person feels himself one with the object of his compassion and identifies himself with that other person.

Non-egoistic actions are thus possible.

This conception, which must give way to Darwin's simpler explanation, can make us aware of how wrong it is to make the non-egoistic sentiment by itself the object of speculation, without attention to the history of its origin. Indeed, the nature of any sensation is clear only to the extent that the history of its origin is also clear.

According to Darwin, non-egoistic behavior is explained in the following way:

Like many animal species, such as bees and ants, our ancestors the apes have a social drive. Brehm says, "The mutual attachment of the members of a tribe (of chimpanzees) is very great. The males love the females, the females their children to a remarkable degree, and the stronger always defend the weaker."[5] This social instinct arises from an extension of the parental instinct and is then maintained and strengthened by natural selection, that is, by the fact that the animal species whose members were most closely bound together by social instincts displaced other species and so continued alone.

As human beings developed from the apes, they thus already had the drive to care for other human beings (at first, of the same community). Someone who has this drive will feel pleasure at seeing other people happy (non-egoistic sympathetic pleasure) and pain at seeing them unhappy (non-egoistic compassion).

Since, however, the strength of this non-egoistic drive is less in most people than the strength of the egoistic drive, this sympathetic pleasure is often undermined by envy, and compassion by malicious pleasure. Often indeed the non-egoistic drive is just as strong as the egoistic drive, or even stronger. Compassion then becomes powerful, and those actions occur that we call sacrificial; one sacrifices one's fortune, health, life, or vanity for others, whereas ordinarily one sacrifices the welfare of others to the egoistic drive, as the stronger.

We have discussed two classes of actions so far: (1) those egoistic actions in which the acting person gains his well-being at the expense of others; and (2) non-egoistic actions in which the acting person, sometimes at the expense of his own well-being, seeks the well-being of others for their own sake or refrains from harming others for their own sake.

Actions of the first kind (which are also called selfish, hard-hearted, lacking in compassion, or even diabolical, when they are based on envy and malicious pleasure) are felt by each of us as morally bad and blameworthy, whereas the second kind are felt as morally good and praiseworthy; and indeed the distinction between "good" and "bad" consists exclusively in these oppositions: *only* egoistic actions are called bad, *only* non-egoistic actions are called good. In fact, whenever we want to pass judgment on the moral value of an action, we investigate its motive and describe the action as morally good only if it has the well-being of others as its motive. Certainly, purely non-egoistic actions are rare; more frequent are actions out of mixed, in part egoistic, in part non-egoistic, motives. In that case, praise is also partial. For example, when it is said that someone has helped others not just out of benevolence, everyone feels that he is praiseworthy only to the extent that he has acted out of benevolence. The degree to which we find a person morally praiseworthy thus corresponds exactly to the degree of his non-egoistic feelings and behavior, so that the best person is the one who lives *only* for others, who indeed gives his life for them. On the other hand, egoism is blamed all the more strongly when it is stronger. For example, someone who destroys the happiness or the life of another for his own advantage is already strongly condemned, but someone who finds no advantage at all in harming them, and harms them only out of envy, only so that they should have no more than himself, displays a state of mind much further removed from benevolence, and he is therefore very strongly condemned.

That only egoism is felt as bad, and only non-egoism as good, also emerges from the following.

The expressions "weakness," "fault," and "vice" are used for those qualities that harm those who possess them. For example, the vanity that makes one feel pain at having displeased is blamed as a weakness; untidiness is blamed as a fault; drunkenness, habitual gambling, and excessive pleasure-seeking are blamed as vices (and also called immorality) because these qualities cause harm to those who possess them. However, someone with such characteristics does not have to be a bad person just for that reason. Rather, the description "bad person" is applied to him only when he does harm not only to himself but also to others by these qualities. For example, the voluptuary will be described as a bad person only if he destroys the happiness of others, such as seducing innocent girls or respectable women to satisfy his passions. On the other hand, if he gives himself over to his passions even in the most unbridled way, but with regard for the happiness of others, he is described as lacking in reason and morals, but not as bad. Similarly, some qualities useful to their owners, such as skill, moderation, courage, and the like (qualities that are often called virtues) are praised because of just this utility, and yet those who do good to themselves by such qualities are not described as good; rather, only those who do good to their fellows, whether by these qualities or by others, are described as good. From this it can be seen that the concept "good person" is used exclusively for the relations of the individual with other people: only the person who cares for others is good, just as the person who harms others is bad.

This comes out with particular clarity in the works of the poets. The good characters there are always those who work for others, and indeed sacrifice themselves for them, such as Posa, whereas the so-called bad characters destroy the welfare of others for the satisfaction of some egoistic drive, such as Richard III (ambition), Iago (vengeance), and the Duke of Alba in *Egmont* (envy).

The question of why egoism is described as bad and non-egoism as good now hardly seems to require an explicit reply. For it is evident that the egoistic behavior that compromises the well-being of one or many members of the community is harmful, whereas non-egoistic behavior is useful. However, it is not only non-egoistic behavior, but often self-interested behavior as well, that is useful to others: for example, a physician who heals for money may achieve as many cures as the physician who helps others out of selfless motives. Similarly, it seems that the security of all is protected just as well when individuals refrain from harming one another out of fear of punishment as when they do the same thing out of benevolence. Nevertheless, neither those who (like the physician) are useful to others so that these others are useful to them in return, nor those who refrain from hurting others out of fear, are described as morally good. Rather, as we have shown, this description is applied only to those who are useful to others, or do not harm them, out of benevolence. So it is necessary to find out why this distinction is made, why only behavior that is useful to others out of *non-egoistic* motives is morally praiseworthy. To explain this, we must go into the nature of punishment as well as that of utility.

Man is a complete egoist, so much so that the members of a tribe of apes are not so hostile to one another as members of a human tribe. For the members of the same tribe of apes are certainly also rivals, but only until their drives for nourishment and mating are satisfied. A human being, in contrast, has not only the drives of hunger and sexuality, which are at least satisfied from time to time, but other insatiable drives as well. He does not only want to eat and drink as well as possible, to live as comfortably as possible, to mate with women as beautiful as possible, and in general to possess goods that are pleasant by themselves: he aspires just as much, and indeed much more, to the possession of goods that, without being pleasant by themselves, produce enjoyment only because one imagines oneself to possess more or to count for more than others. Each person finds himself, so to speak, in competition with others. The person who is less rich wants to overtake the one who is richer, the person who is less respected the one who is more respected, the person who is less celebrated the one who is more celebrated. Nevertheless, however many people he may overtake, there always remain more ahead of him. In this way, the most hostile forms of envy and malicious pleasure have entered into humanity. For we envy those who are ahead of us. In order to overtake them, however, there are two ways: either we achieve more than they, or they lose what they possess. In the second case, whether their misfortune has been brought about by us or by other causes, we feel malicious pleasure.

Apart from this drive of vanity, which animals hardly have at all (see chapter 5), man is also much harder to satisfy than other animals where his natural needs are concerned. For because of the greater development of his intellectual faculties, his so-called reason, he does not concern himself solely, like the animal, with the needs of the moment, but also with those of the future: he wants to possess property. Hence human rivalry is more lasting and intense than rivalry among animals.

These two facts—that each man wants to possess more than others out of vanity, and so is open to hostile feelings of envy and malicious pleasure; and that man takes the future into consideration and therefore, even when the needs of the moment are satisfied, does not want to give up anything he possesses, but instead wants to acquire more and more—have pushed the non-egoistic drive (selfless feelings and behavior) so much into the background that, for example, true friendships, such as that between Orestes and Pylades, belong to mythology.

Apart from this, the instinct that drives us to care for our fellows within the same community, the social instinct, is even with apes only exceptionally as strong as the instinct to care for oneself. The egoistic instinct is the older and stronger, and the non-egoistic instinct is the later and the weaker. We human beings have thus received this non-egoistic instinct from our ancestors as the relatively weaker one; and then it has been completely pushed aside by the desire for property and the effort to have more than others—two drives, of which the first increases self-interest and rivalry, while the second has directly introduced a hostile relationship among humans.

When, in consequence of the evolution of their reason and their vanity, human beings had become as covetous of others' property, as ambitious and envious as we still find ourselves today, a war of all against all must have broken out among them. But that state of affairs would soon have been felt as unbearable and, to put an end to it, people reached for the only means both effective and ready to hand: punishment. Murder or other injuries to members of the same community were subject to punishment, and executive power was conferred upon the person who, owing to his physical strength or his greater cleverness, was recognized as the head of the community. The fear of this punishment kept individuals in restraint, as it still does today. At the same time, property was instituted, in such a way that members of a community divided its territory among themselves.

Thus, after the war of all against all within a community was settled—while the conflicts between different communities continued regardless—the division of labor and the associated exchange of products brought it about that individuals also made themselves useful to one another.

These two forms of egoism, fear of punishment and exchange of products of labor, enable the community to constitute itself as a state.

In this early period, those people were called good who were useful to other members of the community and refrained from harming them, whatever the motives of their actions may have been. Hence Lubbock expressly emphasizes that savages, when they make any moral judgments at all, never consider the motives of actions, but only their usefulness or harmfulness.[6]

Yet at a higher stage in the evolution of knowledge, one must instinctively have felt that, if someone refrains from harming others only out of fear, peace is only imposed from outside and hence exists only on the surface. In fact, anyone who contains his desire to possess the property of others, his hatred, or his desire for vengeance, only out of fear, will seek to satisfy these drives, partly by actions that are not subject to punishment and partly by actions be believes will not be discovered. On the other hand, when people refrain from harming others not out of fear but for their own sake, peace is not imposed artificially from outside but comes from inside. Not only hostile acts but also hostile feelings such as envy and hate disappear; the mind itself is peaceable and peace extends throughout.

Similarly, if someone pursues the well-being of others only as a means to an end, only for his own advantage, this pursuit seems accidental and uncertain. By itself, others' well-being is indifferent to the egoist: he takes account of it only because he cannot achieve his own advantage otherwise. In contrast, for the person who pursues the well-being of others for their own sake, their well-being is not a means but an end; it is prized by itself, and so it is not uncertain but certain, not accidental but necessary. Indeed, if everyone had truly non-egoistic feelings, if everyone loved his neighbor as himself, then communism would not only be possible, it would already be present at hand.*

When people compare such an imaginary state of affairs, in which everyone proves helpful to everyone else for their own sake, with the state actually at hand, in which everyone feels inclined to harm everyone else; and when they feel non-egoistic behavior to be the only thing which could make the complete elimination of hostile relations imaginable, they describe this behavior as desirable, praiseworthy—good.

Thus, non-egoistic behavior would never have been held up as the good if what is at hand coincided with what is desirable, and had always done so, that is, if the non-egoistic drive in human beings were as strong as the egoistic; if it belonged to human nature to care for others as much as for oneself. Some speculative mind may perhaps have arrived at this idea: it would be a good thing if human nature were such that everyone is not concerned only for himself, but just as much for others as well; that he never harbors hostile feelings but only friendly (non-egoistic) feelings toward them. In that case, however, this non-egoism would never have been described as good. For that to occur requires the existence of the bad (egoism): it is just in opposition to this undesirable behavior that non-egoistic behavior is what is desirable, praiseworthy, and good.

Insofar as the degree of non-egoistic feeling and behavior thus became the criterion of moral value, one became used always to looking into motives and to regarding the person who refrains from harming others not out of non-egoistic motives but out of fear of punishment as just as blameworthy as the person who actually does harm others. The action not carried out is morally considered as carried out; for both persons, for example, the murderer and the one who has not committed a murder out of fear of punishment, have an equally low degree of non-egoistic feeling. In the same way, the person who is

---

* The communist's error is taking human beings to be good, when they are bad.

useful to others out of egoism is not described as morally praiseworthy. The action is morally considered as not carried out.

It follows from what has just been said that that the good (non-egoistic) has been praised on account of its utility, because it brings us closer to a state of greater happiness. Nowadays, however, we do not praise the good because of its useful consequences, but instead it appears to us praiseworthy in its own right, independently of all consequences. Although it may originally have been praised on account of its utility, afterward people became accustomed to praising it and forgot that this praise was originally based on usefulness to the community.

One can see this origin of its praiseworthiness very particularly in the following.

Good and useful are used as synonyms, as we will see in further detail in chapter 4, for example, foods, utensils, soldiers are called good when they are useful.

Now, non-egoistic behavior is useful (for the general harmony). It is also praised, and as an expression of this praise, a synonym of "useful" is used, the term "good." The result is that, even if one disregards the historical origin of moral distinctions, the non-egoistic has come to be praised on account of its utility. If this were not the case, we would be able to assert that a certain kind of behavior (the non-egoistic) that is useful and praised and to which a synonym of the word "useful" is applied as an expression of this praise has, despite all this, not come to be praised on account of its utility.

In any case, there must be some reason why non-egoistic behavior is praised; and if a reason as close at hand and clear as the utility of non-egoism is available, it seems superfluous to look around for another.

The same argument applies in a converse way to badness.

Now, it certainly cannot be denied that this theory, which derives the origin of moral distinctions from utility, makes a rather banal impression in art and in life. If indeed badness is based on nothing but the fact that some drive present in human beings (the drive to care for one's fellows, the non-egoistic) has happened to succeed in flourishing only to a slight extent, then the actions themselves, and their presentation in art as well, appear of slight importance. If on the other hand, like Kant and Schopenhauer, different though their points of view were, we claim to glimpse in morality a revelation from the transcendent world, then good and evil gain a deeper significance, as does human behavior and its artistic presentation as well.

A significance that is no doubt too deep: for the explanation of those philosophers is deeper than the object to be explained. Explaining an object too deeply is even worse than explaining it too shallowly. For one will reach the right explanation (that is, the one that has just the same depth as its object) more easily by starting from the shallow explanation than from the one which is too deep. In the first case, one is on the way to the goal and need only go forward, whereas in the second case one has run past the goal and, on recognizing the error, must turn about.

A summary of the first chapter. Everyone cares partly for himself, partly for others.

Anyone who cares for himself at the expense of others is called bad and blamed; anyone who cares for others for their own sake is called good and praised. Such good actions are possible only because we have already inherited from our animal ancestors the drive to care for others.

Egoistic actions that occur at the expense of others were originally condemned on account of their harmfulness; non-egoistic actions were originally praised on account of their utility. Later, the former were condemned in their own right, and the latter praised in their own right.

CHAPTER 2

The Origin of Conscience

Once the distinction had been established between egoistic behavior as bad and non-egoistic behavior as good, people set out to impress it upon children.

Today too this distinction is forced into us from childhood. We constantly hear the selfless person praised and the egoist condemned. The books we read and the plays we see present the same opposition; finally we are directly taught that unselfishness, compassion, benevolence, and sacrifice are good, and that hard-heartedness, envy, and malicious pleasure are bad.

If anyone were raised in exactly the opposite conditions, if from his childhood he heard hard-heartedness, envy, and malicious pleasure called good and praised, and selflessness in contrast called bad and blamed; if it were directly impressed upon him that it is praiseworthy to kill as many as possible of his fellows (from the same state), or else to hurt, annoy, and torment them, whereas it would be bad and blameworthy to give in to the impulses of the non-egoistic instinct and to care for others; if this distinction were also constantly impressed upon him by books and plays, then it would become natural for him to describe the Iagos, Richards, and Gonerils as praiseworthy and good, and the Posas as evil.

The diversity of the customs prevailing in different nations confirms this. For example, anyone raised among a people whose morals allow infanticide will consider that to be as blameless as we consider it to be blameworthy. Again, those like the Indians to whom the murder of strangers has been taught, will feel any such murder to be as praiseworthy as we, to whom the opposite has been taught, consider it to be blameworthy.

Everyone regards as good (or bad) just those actions that he has seen described from his childhood as good (or bad). Indeed, he accepts these distinctions made by his social environment just as insensibly and inescapably as he does the dialect of his social environment.

Once this distinction has been made, however, once someone has become accustomed to connecting the idea of praiseworthiness with a particular mode of action and the idea of blameworthiness with its contrary, it will easily seem to him as if he had not become accustomed to making these connections but had been making them from birth. So it seems to us as if we had been connecting the idea of praiseworthiness with non-egoism and of blameworthiness with egoism since our birth. We are no longer capable of dissociating non-egoism from the idea of praiseworthiness, since we have always seen and thought of them in connection, and similarly for dissociating egoism from blameworthiness. J. S. Mill says excellently, "When we have often seen and thought of two things together, and have never in any one instance either seen or thought of them separately, there is by the primary law of association an increasing difficulty, which may in the end become insuperable, of conceiving the two things apart."[7] But since the understanding of things united by habit depends on separating them, non-egoism must be separated from the idea of praiseworthiness. One must reflect that the two things arise from different sources: non-egoism is innate, an inherited quality of our animal ancestors. The idea of its praiseworthiness, however, developed only at a certain stage of culture and then became, as it now is, a habit acquired by individuals in the course of their lives. Egoism, the drive to care for oneself, is equally innate. However, the description of this drive as bad and blameworthy when it seeks satisfaction at the cost of others—this description developed alongside praise of non-egoism and then became linked by habit with the egoistic drive.

Certainly, the egoistic person, for example, the cruel man, ordinarily appears to us as antipathetic by nature, and the selfless person as sympathetic by nature. If anyone toward whom we are not hostile is treated badly, our compassion is aroused; we feel pain at the fact of his suffering and hence find his assailant unpleasant, disagreeable, and antipathetic. However, this feeling of antipathy must be distinguished from the feeling that makes us call the cruel man bad and blameworthy. This second feeling is the result of a habit and would not occur to an uncivilized person; the first one rests on the innate feeling of compassion and can also be felt by an uncivilized person.

Moreover, if we hate the person treated badly, or if we ourselves have an unusually hard and cruel temperament, the assailant will seem agreeable and sympathetic to us. Nevertheless, we will never call him a good person, and thus it emerges that there is a difference between saying of someone, "He is sympathetic to me, he is antipathetic to me," and saying, "He is a good or evil person." One cannot therefore conclude from the fact that the bad person is often naturally antipathetic to us by nature that moral blame is innate. (Hume in his *Enquiry concerning the Principles of Morals* confuses these two things.[8])

Anyone accustomed to associating the idea of praiseworthiness with non-egoistic behavior and the idea of blameworthiness with egoistic behavior involuntarily associates the satisfying feeling of having done what is good and praiseworthy with his own non-egoistic actions as well, and also associates the painful feeling of having done what is bad and blameworthy with his own egoistic actions.

There is nevertheless a difference, in that the satisfying feeling of having done what is good and praiseworthy is felt at the time of the good action, whereas the painful feeling of having done what is bad and blameworthy follows the bad action. At the moment we act badly, we are so completely occupied by our egoistic drive—our greed, vengefulness, or ambition—that the feeling of the blameworthiness of such an action no longer finds a place in us and remains wholly or almost wholly latent. But once the satisfaction of this instinct has been achieved, whether completely, as in the satisfaction of vengeance, or for the time being, as in the satisfaction of greed or ambition, the memory of the suffering inflicted on another is accompanied at the same time by that painful feeling of having done what is bad and blameworthy.

The more strongly someone feels that egoistic actions are bad, the more he must appear bad and blameworthy to himself when he has been incited by his egoism to commit such actions.

A man who appears bad and blameworthy to himself because he has inflicted suffering on another feels what is called remorse [*sogennante Gewissenbisse*].

Darwin explains remorse differently. He says that we have the drive to care for others. If we are on occasion impelled by egoism not to satisfy this instinct but rather to inflict suffering on others, for example, to kill someone out of greed or fail to relieve his suffering, then when we later recall his suffering (and in any case, the happiness expected from the satisfaction of egoism may perhaps have proven illusory), this drive to care for the other may assert its frustration and manifest itself as a dissatisfied, painful feeling, as remorse.

Such a feeling of frustration must certainly be felt by people when the development of their intellect has enabled them to recall what has occurred in the past whenever they have failed to take account of their non-egoistic instinct. But the feeling of frustration we experience when an instinct—in this case, that of non-egoism—is not satisfied is not remorse, any more than the feeling of frustration we feel when an egoistic instinct is not satisfied, for example, if we have let slip an opportunity to satisfy our vengefulness. Rather, our remorse is characterized by the feeling of blame and self-condemnation—sensations that are comprehensible if we have become accustomed to associating the idea of blameworthiness and condemnation with egoistic actions, such as murder out of greed, and yet which are incomprehensible on Darwin's account (which explains only the feeling of frustration).

The following example, which Darwin uses to illustrate his theory, certainly does suggest that he is correct: if a bird, driven by the migratory instinct to abandon its young, could look back and see them dying of hunger, it would feel pain and remorse over its departure.

In this example, we cannot help supposing that the bird's remorse would consist in feelings of blame and self-condemnation (because our own remorse would involve such sensations in an analogous case). In reality, however, the bird would have only a feeling of frustration owing to the lack of satisfaction of its non-egoistic instinct. For where could it get the idea that such behavior is blameworthy and to be condemned? In the same way, a man who allowed his children to die of hunger—assuming he had never learned that such an action is blameworthy—would have only a feeling of frustration afterward, a compassion coming too late, but not the feelings of blame and condemnation that characterize remorse. This fact seems a paradox to us only because, as has already been said, the blameworthiness of egoistic actions has been taught by everything we have seen, heard, and read from childhood onward, so that we have now become almost incapable of dissociating the ideas of egoism and blameworthiness from one another. We think that they belong together completely and that, therefore, someone who has acted from egoism must have the feeling that his action is blameworthy, that is, must feel remorse, independently of any habits. This belief is false since, as we have shown, remorse is different with different peoples, and each feels remorse over actions that they have been accustomed to regard as blameworthy from childhood.

CHAPTER 3

Responsibility and Freedom of the Will

Remorse differs according to whether whoever feels it bears in mind the necessary character of human actions or not.

First of all, some people think the human will is free, but Hobbes, *Works,* ed. Molesworth, vol. IV, p. 239 et seq.; cf. also his *De Homine,* chap. IX; Spinoza, *Ethics,* First Part, prop. 32; Second Part, last scholium; Leibniz,* in particular his *Theodicy,* I, 166, 167; Wolff, *Psychologica empirica,* para. 889 ff., esp. 925; Hume, *Essay on Liberty and Necessity;* Priestley, *The Doctrine of Philosophical Necessity;* Montaigne, *Essays,* II; Bayle, *Réponse aux questions d'un provinciale,* t. II, p. 116 et seq.; Collins, *A Philosophical Inquiry Concerning Human Liberty;* d'Holbach, *Système de la nature,* esp. I, p. 275; Lamarck, *Philosophie zoologique;* Voltaire, *Le Philosophe ignorant,* chap. 13; Kant, ed. Kirchmann, *Critique of Pure Reason,* p. 436, 438, 442; *Critique of Practical Reason,* p. 115, 116: intelligible freedom is not the subject here; Schopenhauer, *Essay on the Freedom of the Will;* J. S. Mill, *Logic,* II. book 6; Tylor, introduction to *The Origins of Culture;* Bain, *Mental and Moral Science: On Liberty and Necessity;* and others are of the opinion that the human will is not free.

If thinkers such as these say the same thing about a topic for which no new material of observation remains to be discovered, as with an object of the natural sciences, but which is decided rather by sharp observation of material at hand, then this topic can be regarded as settled. For it is impossible to admit that so many observers of the first rank could have made false observations. So it seems superfluous, indeed impossible, to say anything about the nonfreedom of the will that would not have been said already; and if I nevertheless go briefly into this subject, it is more for reasons of completeness than because the topic itself stands in need of any further discussion.

---

* His assertion "Motives incline, but do not compel" has often been misunderstood. What Leibniz means is: however powerfully some motive, for example, a passion, may act upon us, we have the strength to resist it. Such a resistance, however, has particular causes and to that extent occurs with necessity.

Those who maintain the freedom of the will attribute it exclusively to human beings and not to animals as well. Apart from the fact that this is quite inadmissible from the standpoint of the theory of evolution—for at what point in time could the freedom of the will have entered into the descendants of animals?—the same phenomena from which the freedom of the human will is supposed to be deduced are also found in animals.

A dog, for example, hesitates over whether or not to eat forbidden food. He will finally decide to eat it if his appetite is greater than his fear of punishment; otherwise, he will decide in favor of self-control.

In the first case, his action is the necessary consequence of the dominance of appetite. The fact that his appetite dominates is the necessary consequence of the physical and mental state he finds himself in; this state has, however, been brought about by a previous state, and so it goes back to the inherited qualities with which he is born and on which certain influences have acted up to the moment of action.

In the second case, his action is the necessary consequence of the dominance of fear. The fact that this fear dominates is just the necessary consequence of the blows he has received.

Similarly, a man who hesitates over whether he should follow his passion or the ideas of his reason will finally follow his passion if that acts more powerfully on him than the ideas of his reason; otherwise, he will follow his reason.

In the first case, his action is the necessary consequence of the fact that certain influences have acted on the mental and physical qualities with which he was born, in such a way that at the moment of his action, passion was stronger than rational thought.

In the second case, his action is the necessary consequence of the fact that, as a result of (1) the innate constitution of his mind and body and (2) the influences that have acted on these from birth up to the moment of action, a disposition of his mind has been created such that, at the moment of action, despite the strength of passion, the ideas of reason were nevertheless more powerful (otherwise he would in fact have followed his passion).

After the man has acted, however, and perhaps given in to his passion, he thinks: I could have acted differently, and so arises the deceptive illusion that commonly misleads people.

In the first place, if the dog that has eaten the forbidden food were to look backward, he would also think: I could have acted differently. For at the moment of repentance, he feels in himself the capacity to resist his drive to eat, and believes that this capacity was also present in him at the moment when he ate, and that it could also have been effective at that moment. He is right to the extent that the capacity he feels to resist his drive to eat is actually present in his nature—in contrast to, for example, the capacity to fly, which is not in his nature at all. This capacity was also present in him when he ate, just as the capacity to contract is present in a body that expands. But he is wrong when he believes that this capacity to resist his drive to eat could have been effective at the same moment when certain causes (namely, the relatively greater strength of this drive and the relatively lesser strength of fear) drove him to eat—just as, at the same moment when a certain cause forces a body to expand, the body cannot contract in spite of this cause.

The dog does not understand that his capacity to resist could have been effective at that moment only if the state of causes (the strength that his instinct or his fear had at that moment) had been different. He quite fails to see that his capacity to resist can be effective only in virtue of certain causes (thoughts and sensations, which themselves have causes) since every effect must in fact have its cause.

"I could have acted differently" is thus correct, if it is understood to mean: The capacity for acting differently was also in my nature at that time, and my nature could have been swayed by it under other circumstances (that is, if a thought or a sensation had been different). It is false if it is understood to mean: This capacity could have been effective at the time when the state of causes (the thoughts, sensations, and circumstances that were present at precisely that moment, and were themselves produced by certain causes) prevented this effectiveness.

This last, mistaken interpretation of "I could have acted differently" is the interpretation of human beings, as it would be that of the dog capable of recollection. The person who out of two possible actions, for example, walking and running, has chosen one, for example, walking, says, "I could have acted differently" without reflecting that certain causes induced him to choose walking and that, as long as precisely these causes were present, this activity had to follow as well.

This human capacity to choose between various ideas or things is also called "freedom of the spirit," "ability to resist the passions" and "moral freedom." There would be nothing to object to in such expressions if one understood by them only what has been said, and in doing so did not forget that, when someone has chosen one among various things, this choice has been produced by causes that themselves have certain causes, and has therefore occurred with necessity; and that similarly, when someone has resisted his passions, this resistance too is the result of certain causes and so is necessary.

Yet these expressions are misused. Even those who have in fact understood the bondage of the will do not usually dare to utter the proposition "All acts of will are necessary" in public. For they are afraid that those they have punished might say: Why are you punishing me? I had to act in that way. (To which the logical answer would be: I am punishing you so that you will not act the same way in the future, but will have cause to refrain from similar actions out of fear of punishment.) People are afraid of the conclusions of the mob: if everything is necessary, then, giving in to our instincts, we will steal, pillage, and murder (to which the logical response would be: if you give in to your instincts, that occurs in every particular case out of determinate reasons, and so with necessity—and certainly the idea of the necessity of human actions can become the determinate reason for someone to give in to his instincts. But when you are punished so that the fear of this punishment becomes a motive for you to control your instincts in the future, this also occurs out of determinate reasons, and so with necessity, and your crime therefore becomes the determinate reason for your punishment). Because of this fear (often perhaps well-founded) of the bad consequences of the truth (a fear that has impeded the understanding of moral phenomena more than all other obstacles, because someone who is worried by the presentation of a fact because of its consequences does not display it in its true form), our discreet philosophers hide the truth behind the ambiguous expressions "freedom of the mind" and "moral freedom." If they can no longer save the thing itself, they want at least to save the appearance.

To put an end to these absurd disputes, it makes sense to exclude such uses (or rather *mis*-uses) of language as "moral freedom" and the like from the domain of philosophical terminology, and to express oneself instead in ways that are a little longer, but unambiguous.

Even though every act of will is necessary, knowledge of this fact is encountered only in very few people, that is, solely in those who know how to think. All the rest take their will to be free, and so their remorse ordinarily takes the following form. Someone reflects on an action he has committed: for example, Macbeth thinks of the murder of the king and associates the idea of blameworthiness with this action. He then charges himself with this action, in that, without reflecting that it resulted with necessity from the thoughts, sensations, and circumstances present at the moment when it was committed, he thinks unhappily, "I could have acted differently at that moment."

Remorse ordinarily attaches to a single action and retains its sting because we unthinkingly assume the freedom of the will. In most cases, then, remorse is based on an error.

Remorse, however, takes another form with those who understand that all human actions result from causes and therefore result necessarily. This person certainly begins by looking back at an action he has committed and associating the idea of blameworthiness with it. But he does not then charge himself with it by thinking "I could have acted differently." Instead he sees that, as we have said, his action resulted necessarily from certain causes. Among these causes, however, he remarks that the most essential is the constitution of his own character; and now he feels horror at the fact that he has a character from which the actions which he cannot help feeling as blameworthy could proceed. Suppose, for example, that Macbeth could understand that the degree of egoistic feeling present in him at the moment of his action was the sufficient reason for the occurrence of the murder: he would then appear blameworthy to himself, not because he had committed the act, although he could have refrained from committing it, but rather because he was burdened with a character from which such an action could proceed. His remorse, the idea of his blameworthiness, is therefore attached not to the particular act but to its origin in his character, not to the *operari* but to the *esse*—to the fact that he is such a man.

The origin of this horror over the blameworthiness of one's own character is not a mysterious intelligible freedom; we have received our innate character not through any fault of our own; our remorse is not a feeling of regret over the fact that, by virtue of this intelligible freedom, we have chosen just this character and not some better one.

Rather, the origin of this horror is what we have already indicated. In the first place, we have acquired the habit of associating the idea of blameworthiness with egoistic actions such as murder. When we have committed such an act and understand that it has its sufficient reason in the degree of egoistic feeling present in us at the moment of action, we feel horror at having a character capable of blameworthy egoism to such an extent. If we are convinced that our character is innate, then we feel horror at having a blameworthy innate character (i.e., a character from which blameworthy actions have proceeded and may possibly proceed again).

Someone who feels the blameworthiness of his character, his *esse,* does not naturally remark that this feeling is based on habit, that he would not have this feeling of blameworthiness if he had not become accustomed from childhood to regard egoistic actions harming the welfare of others such as murder, as blameworthy. At present he feels only the outcome of habit, that is, he cannot help feeling such actions as blameworthy.

The person on the other hand who has recognized not only that all actions result from causes and so are necessary but also that the label "blameworthy" that we now associate with egoistic actions such as murder has not belonged to them in themselves for all time, but rather (as we will see more fully in the next chapter) that these actions, considered in themselves, are neither condemnable nor blameworthy but actions of a particular nature with which people originally associated the labels "blameworthy" and "condemnable" simply because such actions harm the community—the person who has understood all this will feel remorse, that is, the feeling of his blameworthiness, only weakly, and yet will certainly not be able to avoid it completely. For the habit of associating the idea of blameworthiness with egoistic actions can become so strong that the reflection that says that these actions are not blameworthy in themselves, but have been called blameworthy only because they are harmful to others, will have little resistance against it and be unable to undo the association between the idea of an egoistic action and the idea of blameworthiness.

It is the same in other areas. Someone, for example, who has been powerfully accustomed from childhood to the idea that God exists and that it is sinful to say "The hypothesis of a God is absurd," can seldom utter this proposition in later life without feeling some uneasiness, even if his belief has turned into disbelief. The habit of regarding the ideas of blasphemy and blameworthiness as belonging together can be stronger than the reflection that says that they do not belong together. Similarly, the habit of regarding the ideas of egoism and blameworthiness as belonging together can be stronger than the reflection that says that they do not belong together by nature, but are two things that people have joined together and have done so with their eternal happiness in mind.

Finally, the person who has not at all become accustomed to consider as blameworthy those actions that harm the welfare of others, such as cruelty or murder, will not experience any remorse after committing such actions, as we have already pointed out, but will experience at most a feeling of frustration. A savage, for example, who has cruelly injured one of his tribal fellows, will have a feeling of frustration if his social instinct, his drive to care for others in the same community, is aroused, because he has left that instinct unsatisfied and indeed injured it. But this feeling, stripped of the sensations of responsibility, blameworthiness, and self-condemnation, is nothing but the sort of unsatisfied feeling that arises from the frustration of any drive, and so it cannot be described as remorse.*

Still, anyone who is accustomed to regarding egoistic actions as praiseworthy and non-egoistic actions as blameworthy will experience remorse after having committed non-egoistic actions, as we have already said. If, for example, this distinction had been taught to the Good Samaritan, he would have felt remorse when his non-egoistic instinct had misled him into being compassionate. No doubt he would have had a feeling of satisfaction in conse-

---

* See above, p. 102.

quence of the satisfaction of his non-egoistic instinct; but this would have been negated by the idea of blameworthiness, just as the feeling of satisfaction that arises in us from the satisfaction of an egoistic instinct (e.g., cruelty) is ordinarily negated by the idea of its blameworthiness.

So: the most widespread kind of remorse is that in which the remorseful person appears blameworthy to himself because he has committed a blameworthy action, although he supposes he could have refrained from doing it. In this kind of remorse, we take the will to be free and do not remark that egoistic actions are found blameworthy only out of habit.

Rarer than this is the remorse in which the remorseful person appears blameworthy to himself not because he has committed a blameworthy action he could have refrained from doing, but because such a blameworthy action has proceeded from his character—because he has a blameworthy character. In the case of this remorse, we are convinced of the necessity of human actions. Apart from that, though, we still suppose that egoistic actions are felt as blameworthy by nature, and not out of habit. We do not ask ourselves how we have actually come to regard actions that harm the welfare of others as blameworthy.

Even rarer is the remorse in which the remorseful person has the feeling of blameworthiness only insofar as reflection (which tells him that egoistic actions, regarded in themselves, are not blameworthy by nature but have merely been described by people as blameworthy because of their harmfulness, and that the concept of moral blameworthiness thus produced has then been inculcated into him only by habit) has a weaker influence than the now established habit of considering egoistic actions as blameworthy.

If we were not at all accustomed to finding egoism blameworthy, we would not have any remorse at all after committing egoistic actions.

If, again, we were accustomed to finding non-egoistic actions blameworthy, we would have remorse after committing non-egoistic actions.

Just as we hold ourselves responsible for our actions, so we also hold others responsible for their actions.

Naturally, we attribute the freedom of the will all the more to others. For if, out of two actions possible in themselves, such as a praiseworthy and a blameworthy one, someone has performed the blameworthy action, we think that he could have acted differently. We are correct here, as before, insofar as the capacity to perform the praiseworthy action is in itself present within his nature. But since the blameworthy action has occurred, it must be concluded, considering the principle "every effect has a sufficient cause," that at the moment of the action the sufficient reason of the blameworthy action was present, and consequently the action had to occur.

We thus confuse the capacity that someone generally has to do what is praiseworthy with the capacity to do what is praiseworthy at the moment when the state of causes (thoughts, sensations, and circumstances) brought about the blameworthy action.

Accordingly, we hold others responsible for particular blameworthy actions they have committed, although they were able, as we suppose, to have acted differently.

Holding others responsible is thus based just as much on the error of supposing that the human will is free.

In contrast, when we have understood that every person is born with certain characteristics, that circumstances act on these characteristics, and that certain thoughts and feelings necessarily emerge from the conjunction of these two factors, which in turn necessarily give rise to certain actions—when we have understood the necessity of all human actions, we will no longer hold anyone responsible.

Kant, however, maintains the contrary. He says, "There are cases in which men, even with an education that was profitable to others, have shown from childhood such depravity, which continues to increase during their adult years, that they are held to be born villains and incapable of any improvement in character; yet they are judged by their acts, they are reproached as guilty of their crimes; and, indeed, they themselves find these reproaches as well grounded as if they, regardless of the hopeless quality ascribed to their minds, were just as responsible as any other men."[9]

What Kant means is: when we have recognized that the qualities of character innate in someone are the sufficient reason for his blameworthy actions, we hold him responsible for his innate character.

But this is an error.

In the first place, as we have said, our ordinary way of holding someone responsible has this form: he is responsible because he has committed this blameworthy action, for example, a murder, which he could have refrained from committing. What this overlooks is that the murder, such as the murder of King Edward by Richard III, has its sufficient reason in earlier circumstances that themselves have their causes. On the other hand, whoever has understood that Richard III was born with so much egoism that it could not be diminished by the virtuous admonitions of his educators (which perhaps were beneficial to others) and that this egoism was present in such strength at the moment of the murder that it constituted the sufficient reason for that act—this observer (assuming him not to be a Kantian) would not arrive at the idea of holding Richard III responsible for this innately egoistic personality.

The proposition "tout comprendre est tout pardonner" is correct, although

Kant is actually asserting "tout comprendre n'est pas tout pardonner," which is false.

This notion that people could call one another to account for their innate characters was reinforced in Kant by a false conception of the way people are held responsible, shown in daily experience. He believed, in fact, that this attribution of responsibility included a recognition that human actions are necessary and concluded that it could not apply to the actions recognized as necessary, but solely to their source in innate character. Thus, Kant thought that his doctrine of the attribution of responsibility for innate character was confirmed by daily experience.

If, on the contrary, he had correctly understood the usual attribution of responsibility; if he had remarked that it presupposes the freedom of the will and applies accordingly to particular actions, he would have remarked further that this attribution of responsibility, when the nonfreedom of the will has been understood, does not apply to innate character but ceases to exist, so that daily experience contradicts his doctrine of responsibility for innate character. Furthermore, he would have remarked that the problem of how knowledge of the nonfreedom of the will can coexist with attribution of responsibility does not exist at all, because someone who has recognized the nonfreedom of the will no longer holds anyone responsible.

Hence, he would not have resolved this problem by inventing intelligible freedom or have posited God and immortality with its aid as practical postulates.

CHAPTER 4

The Origin of Punishment and the Feeling of Justice: On Deterrence and Retribution

We discussed the origin of punishment already in chapter 1. We saw there that the welfare and peace of all makes its existence necessary. In fact, if punishment did not exist, if it disappeared at this moment, then each person would snatch as much of the property of others as could be acquired by force, without concern for their happiness or indeed life. The other passions too, such as hate and vengeance, would be pursued without regard for others, unless their defenses frightened us off. For the non-egoistic drive and its forms, compassion and benevolence, are not strong enough to hold egoism in check. Only fear of the power of the state is capable of doing that.

Every state or society is a great menagerie in which fear of punishment and fear of shame are the bars that prevent the beasts from tearing one another to pieces. And sometimes these bars break apart.

After punishment had been introduced to establish peace within a state, the feeling of justice was formed, that is, the feeling on account of which we demand that punishment follow upon bad actions as retribution [*Vergeltung*].

It must be noted that this feeling, which obviously exists in us, does not demand punishment from the same standpoint from which punishment was demanded when it was first established. For the original aim of punishment is, as we have seen, to deter people from bad actions. The feeling of justice, in contrast, does not regard punishment as a means of deterrence for the future, but as retribution for the past. According to this principle, punishment is *quia peccatum est,* not *ne peccetur.*[10]

Nevertheless, the feeling of justice developed out of the original function of punishment and continues to develop even now within each of us during our lives.

The reasoning of the originators of punishment was something like the following. First of all, punishments must be established for bad actions (harming the welfare of one or many members of the community). If this threat is not effective, and someone nevertheless commits an action liable to punishment, that punishment must be inflicted on him, in part because, although the threat of punishment was not enough to deter him, the punishment he now feels will deter him from similar actions in the future, and in part so that his punishment will also be a warning example for others.

Such was the opinion of the lawmakers.

The execution of the judicial decisions delivered at first orally, then in writing, was entrusted to particular people, labeled as "the authorities." These legal administrators had, and have, only the tasks of establishing that the accused person actually committed the crime he is charged with, of checking in the legal statutes what punishment is set down for the crime in question, and of carrying out this punishment. They concern themselves therefore only with the bad action that has been committed and its punishment. However, whether this punishment is a reminder for the future or a retribution for the past— understandably, consideration of this puzzle does not occur to them. Neither they nor others recall the original aim of the punishment.

But if nothing in the punishments carried out reminds one that they are a means of deterrence for the future, it must come to seem that they are a retribution for the past. Suppose that someone is punished for theft. According to the original intention of punishment, this punishment is supposed to deter the thief himself and everyone else from similar actions. This future-directed meaning of punishment does not, however, emerge clearly from the punitive process. The judges merely assert that, under these circumstances, this punishment must be inflicted for theft, and they then carry it out. It seems therefore that they are punishing not to prevent other thefts, but because of the theft already committed; they seem to be taking retribution for the theft already committed.

Because nothing reminds the judges, the accused, and the spectators of the original meaning of the punishment, they become accustomed to see it as what it seems to be, a retribution.

But since retribution has always, as one supposes, been seen to follow lawless actions, then whenever one sees a lawless action, one involuntarily has the feeling that some retribution must follow upon it—that is, the feeling of justice.

If instead of this, one reflected on each occasion of punishment that it is not, as it seems, for retribution but for deterrence, and that therefore the formula of punishment, "You are punished because you have done this" must be understood *cum grano salis*, not as meaning "You are punished because of the action itself," but as meaning "You are punished so that actions such as you have committed will not be committed again, either by you or by others"; if the future-directed meaning of punishment were kept in people's minds, then nobody would come to have the feeling of justice. But since this indication is not usually given, punishment must seem to be retribution and thus gives rise to the feeling of justice.

Another circumstance adds to this. When we are punished as children, it is obviously not as a retribution for our misbehavior but rather to prevent its return. Yet we are told, "You are being punished because you have done this." So from childhood onward we have the impression that punishment is retribution, and this feeling is developed further by everything we see and hear about legal punishment.

Apart from the fact that the punishments carried out by authorities and educators have the appearance of being acts of retribution for bad actions, another error contributes to the formation of the feeling that leads us to demand retribution for bad actions.

As we have already said, the human will is believed to be free. "The criminal deserves punishment because he has acted in such a way, although he could have acted differently."

If, however, the necessity of criminal actions had been understood, the idea that retribution must be carried out for them would not have been able to gain a footing. Rather, one would have rightly said: Actions that are necessary cannot be subjected either to attribution of responsibility or to retribution for what has occurred; rather, it is precisely because they are necessary, that is, determined by certain motives, that punishment should be applied to them, so that the fear of this punishment becomes a motive for the agent himself and everyone else to refrain from such actions in the future.

The feeling of justice thus arises out of two errors, namely, because the punishments inflicted by authorities and educators appear as acts of retribution, and because people believe in the freedom of the will.

Once this feeling has arisen, it is applied not only to the bad actions that are discouraged by the law or by educators entrusted with punishment; but is also applied, owing to acquired habits, to *all* actions taken to be bad. In the face of any blameworthy action, the feeling now arises that some retributive suffering should follow. Accordingly, whenever some bad action leads to suffering for the person in question, people say it is a deserved punishment for him, the just deserts of his badness.

Indeed, even when suffering comes not *out of* a bad action but simply *after* it (e.g., when someone who has acted badly is later killed by a falling roof tile), the habit of demanding retribution for a bad action makes people consider this mere succession of events as a causal process, and they say, "The Lord, whose ways are marvelous, has inflicted this suffering on the bad man as punishment."

Even the hypothesis of a punishment after death, although it was invented in part with the intention of deterring people from bad actions, rests in another part on what we have already said. Since we see many bad actions go unpunished in the world (for whether the evildoers undergo suffering in consequence of their bad actions depends on the accidental formation of circumstances) and since we have also now acquired the idea that suffering must be the consequence of evildoing, it is easy to add the superstition that transfers the missing punishment into a future life, which has already been assumed for other reasons.

Is legal punishment a deterrent for the future or a retribution for the past?

The reply to this question is often: the feeling present in us that makes us demand retribution for crimes proves that such retribution does actually occur and that legal punishment must therefore be understood as retribution.

This could be said for as long as the origin of the feeling of justice remained unknown. Now that we have understood that this feeling is a consequence of two errors and has arisen from an illusion, it follows immediately that this feeling, which tells us that the criminal must meet with retribution, is not respectable, that it lies. In fact, one must not punish because a bad action has been committed, but so that a bad action will not be committed. *Nemo prudens punit, quia peccatum est, sed ne peccetur.*[11]

Thus, if punishment exists to deter people from committing harmful actions, for the well-being of all, and actions harming the well-being of one or many citizens are accordingly punished so that they will not be repeated, it follows that the more someone harms the well-being of others, the more he and all others must be deterred from repeating similar actions. The greater the crime (the harm to others), the greater the punishment. Whoever commits the greatest harm to others, that is, murder, must be completely excluded from the community for its own good, partly because, as far as he himself is concerned, one cannot risk allowing him to return to his actions, but also partly because the other citizens must be deterred from such great crimes by such great punishments. Whether this exclusion from the community must be applied in the form of lifelong imprisonment or the death penalty has to be decided by statistics. If the lifelong imprisonment of murderers is just as effective as the death penalty in protecting the general well-being, that is, if murders do not become more common with the abolition of the death penalty, then the death penalty is unjustified. If on the other hand imprisonment is a lesser deterrent than the death penalty, that is, if murders become more common with the abolition of the death penalty, then the well-being of all requires its maintenance. It is reasonable to destroy the life of a few in order to preserve the life of many.

(This can be compared with Hobbes's theory of deterrence in his *Leviathan*: "Punishment is an evil inflicted on the transgressor of the law by public authority, to the end that the will of citizens may be disposed to obedience from terror of it."[12] Plato says in his *Protagoras*, "But he who desires to inflict rational punishment does not retaliate for a past wrong which cannot be undone; he has regard to the future, and is desirous that the man who is punished, and he who sees him punished, may be deterred from doing wrong again."[13] Spinoza, Beccaria, Schopenhauer, Feuerbach, and almost all of the theoreticians of jurisprudence say the same thing.)

The rightness of punishment thus does not rest on the feeling of justice; rather, punishment of any wrongdoer is justified only in consideration of the common good. The end (the common good) justifies the means (punishment). Nevertheless, people condemn the proposition "The end justifies the means." Everyone takes it to be blameworthy. Even the Jesuits do not acknowledge it openly.

If it were genuinely blameworthy, its application must also be blameworthy, so it appears necessary to put it to the test.

In the proposition "The end justifies the means," the verb "justify" indicates that a morally good end is meant. It follows from our discussion that only the person who seeks the well-being of others for their own sake has such an end.

Let us suppose now that someone can attain his good end only by inflicting suffering, but that this suffering is less than that which would occur without his intervention. Such a case is that of a man who seeks the well-being of his fellow citizens for their own sake, but who can attain this end only by the assassination of a particular citizen. Here two evils are given, of which one is necessary. Either the whole people perish, or a single person perishes. When someone chooses the lesser of these two evils and kills the single person, the motive for his action is reasonable, good, and praiseworthy.

It may perhaps be objected that the agent cannot know in advance with any certainty whether committing his act will actually have such good consequences, or whether refraining from it will have such bad consequences. This is correct but irrelevant. For morality does not look at the outcome, but at the agent's intention or motivation. It is sufficient when the agent has the conviction that the dilemma indicated—either a whole people must perish, or a single individual—does in fact exist.

Hence, someone who has the good aim of preventing or eliminating the unhappiness of others, and who can attain this end only by producing a relatively smaller unhappiness (or believes this) is morally justified in using this means for attaining his end. His end justifies his means.

Daily life offers us innumerable examples in which this principle is recognized as correct and followed. The physician inflicts sufferings on the invalid for healing; often he cannot avoid lying to the patient. The educator too often finds himself in the situation of having to lie to his pupils. Even Plato elevates the lie to the rank of a law of his ideal state, in the case where the end is a good one.[14]

One should not forget that, as we have said, it is never a question here of the consequences that in fact result from the use of means that are blameworthy in themselves. The agent is morally justified as long as, according to his knowledge and his conscience, the means he uses are the lesser of two evils.

Certainly justification in terms of morality is quite different from justification in terms of the law. Even when someone uses blameworthy means not only with a good intention but also in fact prevents or eliminates a greater evil through them, the state cannot allow him to go unpunished if he breaks a law. If it did, the authority of the law would suffer. The crowd would not see the good intention there but only the lack of punishment and so would be encouraged, and even think itself justified, in also acting against the law. In this way the peace of all, maintained solely by fear of punishment, would be endangered. Hence, the state can certainly recognize extenuating circumstances but cannot grant immunity from punishment.

The same principle that justifies the means used by the individual person authorizes the state to punish: in both cases the end (prevention of a greater evil) justifies the means (producing a relatively smaller evil).

The proposition "The end justifies the means" is thus valid—as long as the conditions, to be mentioned once again, are satisfied:

(1) The end must be a good one.

(2) Even if the end is good, it does not justify means that cause suffering unless it cannot be achieved in any other way. It is imaginable that someone who seeks the well-being of others for their own sake uses means that give rise to suffering to achieve this end, whether for convenience or for other reasons, although he knows that other means are available to him.

(3) If this good end is achieved by the use of means that cause suffering, only those means are justified which, under the circumstances, produce the least possible suffering. The previous example applies here too, mutatis mutandis. According to this principle, the death penalty is unjustified in states where life imprisonment is an equally great deterrent against murder.

(4) The suffering that is produced must be less than that which would occur without these means. It is, for example, unjustified to take the life of many people in order to save the life of a single person, whereas it is justified to take the life of a single person if this alone will save the lives of many people.

It is still necessary to indicate the reasons for the condemnation of our proposition, in accordance with Aristotle's principle that one should uncover not only the truth but also the reasons for the error which corresponds to the truth.

First of all, nearly all those who reject the proposition "The end justifies the means" have never reflected on it. They condemn it because from childhood on they have been told frequently and insistently that it is to be condemned. Their condemnation is a *pre*-judice, since it is based not on an examination but on a habit that *pre*-cedes any examination.

Hence, they do not have this opinion because they take it to be true: they take it to be true because they have it.

Since habit—which is the foundation of almost all opinions, especially religious ones—firmly associates the idea of blameworthiness with the idea of the proposition "The end justifies the means," they are astonished when they encounter someone who does not associate the idea of blameworthiness with that of this proposition.

Even after their astonishment, they still do not concede a single doubt as to the correctness of their own opinion, partly because reflection is required to resolve such doubts, and partly because they cannot concede that the other person's opinion could be correct—that he could be in the right—that they themselves could have been in the wrong for so long. For this reason, they pass directly from their astonishment into the assurance that they are in the right and the other in the wrong.

It may perhaps be said: granted that the opinion that our proposition is to be condemned has been acquired and asserted by many people, how did the proposition originally fall into discredit?

For two reasons: because it has been misunderstood, and because it has been misused.

It is misunderstood by those who cite cases where the four conditions stated are not satisfied. The first condition in particular is often overlooked; many people whose end is not a good but an egoistic one and who use bad means (that is, harm the welfare of others) to achieve it, advance the proposition "The end justifies the means" as their justification. Obviously, such an interpretation contradicts the sense of the proposition since, as we have said, the word "justify" clearly shows that what is meant is a good end.

Our proposition has been misused by the Jesuits and Inquisitors who acted as if they had a good end, when in fact their end was a bad one. They claimed that heretics had to be burned so that all the rest of humanity, contaminated by them, should not be subject to eternal damnation.

Let us suppose they were right: in that case, their behavior would deserve praise. For it is reasonable to burn one part of humanity in this world to prevent all of humanity from burning eternally in the afterlife. Or suppose that they at least believed they were right: in that case, their motive would have been a good one, and their behavior morally justified. However, they were not right, nor did they believe that they were right: they merely pretended to act out of love of God and humanity; they acted in fact out of love of themselves, since, as everyone knows, they acted out of ambition and greed in burning those who threatened their power by adopting a new religious confession. Hence, their end did not justify their means. But since they appealed to the proposition "The end justifies the means," this proposition took on an unpleasant aftertaste of burning: since then, anyone who hears it uttered cannot help thinking of the burning of heretics.

Since our proposition cannot prevent itself from having been in part misunderstood and in part misused, we can acknowledge its correctness without worrying about these facts.

The state's justification in punishing falls under this proposition. For the state is like a person who wants the well-being of the people but who can achieve this good end only by using means that produce suffering, that is, by punishing those who break the law. The suffering that results is less than that which would have occurred without the use of these means. For punishment affects the well-being only of the individuals who commit offences, whereas without the use of punishment the well-being of all would suffer, and the *bellum omnium contra omnes* would occur.

We have seen in this chapter that punishment was originally introduced in order to deter people from bad actions, and that the feeling arose later that it is necessary to punish not only as deterrence against bad actions but as retribution for them. We saw further that this feeling, since it arose as an error, must not be taken into consideration, and that no criminal must be punished for his crime by itself.

Let us now examine this truth, that nobody deserves blame or punishment because of his bad actions by themselves, from another, highly important standpoint.

Human beings find themselves in the midst of a world containing various things, some useful to them, others useless or harmful.

The things useful to us we often call good, and the things useless or harmful, bad. For example, good food is food suitable for human beings; good land is that which bears abundant crops consumable by human beings; good horses are useful horses. In the same way, bad foods are those that are not good for us, and so on.

It can be said in general, wherever the adjective "good" (or "bad") is linked with a noun, it means that this object is useful (or harmful). This becomes especially clear when one tries to apply the words "good" or "bad" to objects which have no relation to our use or harm: for example, "a good star" sounds senseless, because fixed stars cannot be divided into stars that are useful to us and others that are useless or harmful to us. Similarly, "good dust" would be senseless for anyone who does not know that road dust has a use, namely, for the manufacture of artificial marble. In contrast, the manufacturers will describe as good any dust that is good for this manufacture, and vice versa. Thus, good is the same as useful, bad the same as useless or harmful.

Therefore one should really not say, "This object is good," but only, "This object is good for me." Even when something, such as a moderate heat, is beneficial to all human beings, one should really not say, "Moderate heat is a good temperature," but rather, "Moderate heat is a temperature that is good for all human beings."

Owing to an imprecise mode of expression, ordinary language attaches the relations that things have to us to the things themselves, as predicates.

What has been said about the predicates "good" and "bad" applies to the predicates "beautiful" and "ugly," "hard" and "soft," "hot" and "cold," "white" and "black," and all the others that Locke called secondary qualities.[15] Nobody believes, for example, that vermilion has a red color in itself, independently of beings provided with appropriate optical nerves.

> A person who is red-blind will see vermilion as black or as a dark gray-yellow. This too is the correct reaction for an eye formed in the special way his is. All he has to know is that his eye is simply formed differently from that of other persons. In itself the one sensation is not more correct and not more false than the other, although those who call this substance red are in the large majority. In general, the red color of vermilion exists merely in so far as there are eyes which are constructed like those of most people. Persons who are red-blind have just as much right to consider that a characteristic property of vermilion is that of being black.[16]

Nevertheless we say, "Vermilion is red" and not "Vermilion is red for us," just as we say, "Moderate heat is a good temperature" instead of "Moderate heat is a good temperature for us."

Thus, it is as completely senseless to call an object taken by itself good as it is to call vermilion taken by itself red: it is just for beings provided with certain sensory nerves that the vermilion is red and something like moderate heat is good. For beings provided with somewhat different sensory nerves, the vermilion would be yellow, and moderate heat or anything else that we call good would be bad.

Spinoza writes in his *Ethics:* "We see that all the notions the crowd use to explain nature [i.e., good and evil, order and confusion, heat and cold, beauty and ugliness, etc.] are modes of the imagination and indicate, not the nature of anything, but only some constitution of the imagination."[17] And: "As for good and evil, they are nothing positive in things considered as it were in themselves, but indicate nothing other than modes of thought or notions."[18]

If after these introductory remarks we return to moral good and evil, what we have said remains valid. Let us recall first of all the origin of the concepts good and bad, as this was described in the first chapter.

In the beginning, people called good that which was useful to others (members of the same community) and bad that which harmed them. Later, they took account not just of whether someone was in fact useful, but of the motives of his actions, and they called good only those actions useful to others that were carried out from non-egoistic motives (that is to say, for the sake of the others). Motives begin to be examined because, when people help or refrain from harming others out of egoistic motives (such as self-interest and fear of punishment) their accord is accidental, insecure, and externally enforced, whereas if they help or refrain from harming one another out of non-egoistic reasons, their accord is secure, solid, and comes from within.*

Non-egoistic behavior is thus called good because it is useful (for achieving social accord), and egoistic behavior is called bad because it is harmful.

Just as a moderate temperature, although it is called good by human beings because it is pleasant to their sensory nerves, is, considered by itself, neither good or bad but just a temperature of a certain nature, so too the non-egoistic person, although he is called good by others because he is useful to them, is nevertheless, considered by himself, not a good person but just a person of a certain nature. To call the non-egoistic person considered by himself good would make no sense, just as it is senseless to call a moderate temperature considered by itself good, or vermilion considered by itself red.

Similarly the egoistic person, for example, the cruel person, although he is called bad by his neighbors because he harms them, is nevertheless, considered by himself, not a bad person but just a person of a certain nature. It would be senseless to call a cruel person considered by himself bad.

---

* See above, pp. 96–97.

Let us take yet another analogy: the good person is a useful animal, the bad person is a harmful animal.

Just as any other harmful animal, such as a vicious dog, is bad because he is bad for human beings, yet considered by himself is not bad but just an animal of a certain nature, so too the cruel person is bad because he is bad for human beings, yet considered by himself he is not bad but just a person of a certain nature.

This analogy, which is in fact complete, seems incomplete to us. For the vicious dog is felt to be bad owing to his harmfulness, and not owing to his inner nature. In contrast, the cruel person is felt to be bad owing to his inner nature, independently of the fact that others are harmed by him.

This difference is based on the following. Although cruelty and similar kinds of behavior were originally called bad because they are bad for others, in later generations this reason for the designation was not kept in mind, but only the designation itself was maintained out of habit. Suppose someone is asked why cruelty is bad. He will answer: because he feels it is bad. If one inquires into the origin of this feeling, one finds the habit according to which cruelty has been presented to him as bad in itself by everything he has heard, seen, and read from childhood onward. If one inquires further into the first origin of this designation of the behavior in question, one encounters a distant level of culture in which cruelty and similar kinds of behavior were first described as bad, not because they were regarded as bad in themselves, but because they were bad for others. As we have said, this reason was forgotten by later generations since, like us, they were simply taught (i.e., without being given a reason) that cruelty and other similar behaviors are bad. In this way, it came to seem, as pointed out, that cruelty is bad in itself and not just bad insofar as it is harmful to others, like the viciousness of the dog.

The analogy described above is indeed complete: just as the vicious dog considered in itself is not bad but just an animal of a certain nature, so too the cruel person considered in himself is not bad but just an animal of a certain nature. It is senseless to call cruelty considered in itself bad, just as it is senseless to describe as bad in itself an extreme temperature or anything else that is bad just for human beings.

So if cruelty and egoistic behavior in general, considered in themselves, are not bad but just behavior of a certain nature, then this behavior considered in itself cannot be liable to blame, punishment, or retribution. Instead, just as we lock up or kill vicious dogs, although they do not deserve punishment, so too we will condemn, lock up, and sometimes kill individuals who are harmful to others (thieves, murderers) even though they do not deserve punishment, so that the fear of punishment may become a motive for them and everyone else not to harm others again.

From this standpoint too, punishment is not retribution but deterrence.

Let us recapitulate the contents of this chapter by an example. If someone commits a murder for theft, the naïve spectator says: His action is bad in itself and it deserves (the feeling of justice adds) retribution in the form of punishment. The criminal is responsible (thoughtlessness comments) because he could have acted differently, since his will is free.

In contrast, the thinking spectator will say: (1) It is senseless to call that action considered in itself bad; considered by itself it is an action of a certain nature. This action appears to us bad in itself because we have become accustomed from our childhood to find such actions bad in themselves. (2) This action does not deserve retributive punishment, in part because it is not bad considered in itself, and in part because the feeling on account of which we demand retribution has arisen from errors. Punishment is justified only for deterrence, and on the basis of the proposition "The end justifies the means." (3) The murderer is not responsible at all, since his action results with necessity from his innate character and the impressions that have influenced him from his birth up to the moment of action.

Anyone who has arrived at only one of these three insights holds no one responsible; however, as the majority of people do not arrive at any of these three insights, they hold everyone responsible.

In view of these observations, the hypothesis of eternal retribution mentioned earlier appears all the more inadmissible. For:

(1) It presupposes the existence of God. The untenability of this hypothesis has been decisively shown by Kant.

(2) Even conceding the existence of God, predicates such as "good" and "bad" could not be attributed to him. "God is good" would mean: God does good to the world and its inhabitants. "God is bad" would mean: God does harm to the world and its inhabitants. But since all we know of the world is our small globe, and nothing of God, there is no basis for calling him good or bad.

(3) If one nevertheless wants to attribute one of the predicates "good" or "bad" to God, it will obviously have to be the predicate "bad," for all the beings we know (especially human beings) have many sufferings and few pleasures. Accordingly, the god of the savages who, still untroubled by theological subtleties, assume a malevolent cause for the many evils they feel, is an evil demon.

(4) If God is taken as perfectly good, despite what we have said, he cannot at the same time be cruel, let alone crueler than the most hard-hearted of mortals. Even such a person would finally be satisfied by the continually prolonged sufferings of his victim. In contrast, this God of perfect goodness inflicts the endless torments of Hell, and does so even though he is himself the ultimate cause of everything that exists, and therefore even of bad actions.

(5) This hypothesis presupposes the existence of a soul. But the differences between the higher animals and human beings are not so great that one could attribute a special soul to human beings.

(6) Even if we do concede the existence of a soul, this soul cannot be the victim of torments, since it is immaterial.

(7) The actions for which God inflicts this retribution do not actually deserve retribution (see the preceding).

It is not difficult to discover the origin of these assumptions: after the personification of natural forces was abandoned, the existence of God was deduced from the cosmological and teleological arguments (refuted by Kant). Having arrived at the existence of God, our theologians provide him with the predicate of perfection, which includes perfect goodness. Yet this perfect goodness cannot deter us from bad actions; indeed, we may well rely upon it and lose all fear and all respect for God himself and for his representatives on earth as well. Partly for this reason, but also because, as we have already said, because the feeling of justice leads us to demand a retributive punishment in the beyond for bad actions unpunished in this life, the God of perfect goodness is also cruel—an eternal avenger. Finally, the hypothesis of a soul detachable from the body arose originally from dreams (see the works of Tylor and Lubbock).[19] Savages believe they have actually lived through what they have dreamed, for example, that they have actually met a person they met in a dream. But since their body has not left its place, as they see on awakening and others confirm, something separable from the body must have undertaken this travel. In death, the soul separates itself completely from the body, just as it is temporarily separated from it in sleep.

So it is that belief in a retribution after death was able to arise. That this is still believed by theologians today is explained by the fact that they are only rarely in the habit of reexamining what has been taken as true in their church. It is not in human nature, as ordinarily found, to risk one's peace of mind out of a relentless regard for truth* (and this peace of mind is usually very great with blind faith) or to place one's situation and income in jeopardy by admitting the truth.

---

* Relentlessness is the virtue of philosophers.

CHAPTER 5

The Origin of Vanity*

It is not a matter of indifference to us whether others have a good or bad opinion of us for two main reasons: (1) because we are self-interested, and so hope for advantages from a good opinion, and are afraid of disadvantages from a bad opinion; (2) because we are vain, so that a good opinion is itself pleasant and a bad opinion is itself unpleasant.

Vanity thus has a positive and a negative aspect: we hope for a good opinion, that is, to please, to be admired and envied; we are afraid of a bad opinion, that is, of displeasing, of being discredited, despised, or mocked.

For example, we want to please by our appearance, personality, and behavior: we want it said of us that we are beautiful and amiable and that we know how to behave. We hope especially to attract admiration and envy by our mental successes, such as our literary works; or again by the extent of our physical successes: we want to withstand and be able to endure more than others. In order to attract admiration or envy, we use all the relevant advantages of mind, body, or external goods (riches, distinction, high position, etc.). On the other hand, it is painful to us to displease, to be regarded as physically or mentally weak or as a coward, or to be discredited and despised because of some lack of mental, physical, or external advantages.

This positive aspect of vanity is divided into vanity in the narrower sense and ambition. It is characteristic of the person who is vain in the narrower sense that he wants to please, to be admired and envied now, whereas the person who is called ambitious is the one who first sets out to acquire the advantages that excite admiration and envy. The qualities by which we please (grace, beauty) would be an object of ambition if they could be acquired by the power of the will alone.

The negative aspect of vanity is designated by everyday language as the sense of honor. So it is said of the person for whom discredit and contempt (dis-

---

* In this chapter some material is borrowed from the author's *Psychological Observations.*

honor) is painful, indeed unbearable, that he has a sense of honor, and of those who are indifferent to this shame that they do not have a sense of honor.

Remark. The word "vanity" is used here in a wider sense than the usual one. We usually describe as vain only those in whom the desire to please, to possess more than others, or to be admired is immediately evident (in other words, those who are described here as vain in the narrower sense), and we distinguish from them the ambitious and those who act out of a sense of honor. However, vanity in the narrower sense, ambition and the sense of honor are, as we have shown, expressions of the same fundamental drive, namely, concern for the opinion of others for its own sake (in contrast with concern for the opinion of others owing to the utility one expects from it: that is, from self-interest). The difference simply consists in whether this concern shows itself immediately, in which case it is called vanity; or whether it appears in the form of work aimed at acquiring the advantages that excite admiration and envy: in which case it is called ambition; or whether it appears in the form of a sensitivity to contempt (to dishonor): in which case it is called the sense of honor. The author has no intention whatever of expressing a general condemnation in labeling these different forms of the same basic instinct as vanity, a word taken to have connotations of blame. He does not want to present something like, for example, the sense of honor, which people ordinarily consider to be praiseworthy, as something blameworthy in his eyes. Rather, he uses the word "vanity" just to have a single expression for the psychological phenomenon he is about to explain, namely, concern for the opinion of others for its own sake. To what extent and for what reasons people condemn this concern will be examined later.

The existence of vanity is a problem: Why is admiration agreeable to us, even when we do not expect any advantages resulting from it? Why is contempt painful to us, even when we do not expect any disadvantages resulting from it?

The explanation of these phenomena has been sought in the fact that admiration brings to our mind the value or utility of what is admired (e.g., practical intelligence), whereas contempt brings to mind the harmfulness of what is despised (e.g., stupidity). Yet the person who takes pleasure in admiration not for its own sake but only insofar as it brings to his mind the value of what is admired, is not called vain. That label is given rather to the person who takes pleasure in possessing a quality because he can obtain admiration by it. Similarly, it is not the person who suffers from contempt only insofar as this contempt brings to mind the harmfulness of what is despised who feels wounded in his honor; rather, it is the person who suffers from contempt itself and is pained by some defect or other only insofar as it brings contempt upon him. To explain these phenomena correctly, we need to draw upon analogies in the animal kingdom.

With bird species where the number of males is greater than the number of females, there occurs, according to Darwin, a competition of the males for possession of the females (sexual selection). Male singing birds, for example, engage in a contest of song in the presence of the female, and she then chooses the best singer. In this way, it is always just the best singers who leave descendants behind, and since their descendants inherit their singing ability, male singing birds thus acquire little by little their beautiful singing. However, they practice the art thus achieved not only for that particular end but also, once accustomed to exercising it, without any definite end: one often hears birds competing in their singing without intending to gain possession of a female.[20]

The same thing applies to birds that court their female not by singing but by displaying their plumage. This is how peacocks have acquired their magnificent plumage, because the females always prefer the most beautiful among them, who pass on their qualities. However, once the peacocks had become accustomed to seeing their spread plumage admired during courtship, they also found pleasure in this admiration by itself, out of established habit; the peacock likes to spread his plumage before his fellows and before other animals, even before pigs (according to Darwin), and he visibly takes pleasure in the feeling of being admired.

Thus, instincts originally acquired for a particular end, such as the instinct that originally led a peacock to having his plumage admired during courtship, often come into play independently of that end.

If we return to our problem with this insight, its solution is now simple. That is:

When people began to live together in communities, the individual often had an advantage in pleasing persons of the other sex, or persons of his own sex. Similarly, it was often useful to him that his achievements, for example, the weapons he made, were admired by others, in case he wanted to exchange them for other objects. Just as the peacock originally found pleasure in knowing his plumage to be pleasing and admired—on account of utility (the possession of the female) but later, out of acquired habit, also found pleasure in this by itself—so too human beings originally found pleasure in knowing their person or their achievements to be pleasing and admired, on account of some utility, but later, out of acquired habit, also found pleasure in this by itself.

The difference between the peacock and the human being is in the following. Since, of all the peacock's mental or physical qualities, his plumage is the only one for which pleasing and being admired is useful to him, it follows that his plumage is the only one for which (out of acquired habit) pleasing and being admired is agreeable to him by itself; the peacock is vain only of his plumage. A human being, on the other hand, has an advantage from pleasing and being admired not just for his appearance, but also for his strength, courage, intelligence, weapons, and so on. Indeed, the situations in which the opinion of others is important for him are so many and varied that he can sometimes find utility in being admired for any physical, mental, or external quality, or be harmed by being despised or scorned for them. Owing to acquired habits, the fact that any one of his qualities is admired is agreeable to him by itself, while its being despised is disagreeable to him by itself. Human beings are vain of every one of their qualities, even if not to the same extent. On this point, the male sex differs from the female sex: man is vain first and foremost of his intelligence, courage, and strength, and only in the second place of his beauty. Woman, in contrast, is vain first and foremost of her beauty, and only well afterward, to some extent, of her other qualities. This difference is to be explained as follows.

However the different forms of marriage, communal marriage, polyandry, polygamy, and monogamy may have developed from one another (the historians writing about marriage are not in agreement on this), the custom for many generations before us has been that, unlike the case with singing birds and peacocks, it is women who present themselves for choice by the men: the woman does not choose a man, but the man chooses one or several women, as beautiful as possible. It is therefore just as important for the woman as for the peacock to please the other sex, and to distinguish herself by her beauty. Indeed, it is even more important for woman to win a man than for the peacock to win the female, because she finds in man not only the satisfaction of her sexual need, but also lifelong support for herself and her children; hence it is even more important for woman to be beautiful than for the peacock. No doubt beauty is not the only quality by which woman can please: women supplement their beauty as much as possible with amiability, intelligence, efficiency and, especially in our time, with money. Despite all this, it is always beauty that makes the greatest impression on a man.

Mindful of the utility of their beauty, therefore, women have always associated a great sense of pleasure with the feeling of being beautiful or pleasing and a great sense of displeasure with the feeling of being ugly or displeasing. However, if a strong sense of pleasure always arises from the feeling of being beautiful or pleasing, at first with the utility of beauty in mind, then later on, whenever there is the feeling of being beautiful, a strong sense of pleasure will persist out of habit, even without the utility of beauty in mind—just as the peacock found pleasure in admiration of his beauty at first out of utility but then also by itself. The same reasoning in reverse applies to ugliness and to displeasing.

Women thus aspire to please and be admired by men for their beauty, not only because they would like to marry one of them but because, as we have said, they feel a strong sense of pleasure whenever they please and an even stronger sense of displeasure whenever they displease. When this desire to please comes into view in glances, gestures, and ways of showing or hiding one's charms, the woman is called a coquette. A woman who not only does not *seem* to want to please, but in fact does not want to please, would be a rare exception because, owing to these circumstances, the desire to please is one of the strongest drives of the female sex.

Whereas the vanity of women, like that of peacocks, is essentially limited to their plumage, the vanity of man is, as we have said, not limited exclusively to his external aspect. For, since he is not chosen but himself makes the choice, as the females of the peacocks and singing birds do, beauty is not very important for him.

Certainly it sometimes happens that the woman chosen by a man refuses him by reason of his ugliness, despite the advantages she could expect from that marriage; in general handsome men do have a greater prospect than ugly ones of winning women, especially beautiful women. Hence even men, with the utility of beauty in mind, are accustomed to associate a sense of pleasure with the idea of being beautiful, of pleasing and being admired for their beauty. If, however, the idea of being admired for one's beauty is often followed by a sense of pleasure, then later on, the occurrence of the first feeling will be involuntarily followed by the second as well, even when there is no question of the utility of beauty: being admired for one's beauty is agreeable to a man by itself, and so man too is vain of his external aspect, even if to a lesser degree than woman.

More useful, however, to a man than being admired for his beauty (even for winning a woman) is being admired for his strength, his courage, his intelligence, and his achievements. For through recognition of these qualities he acquires a privileged, advantageous position among his fellows. In consequence of this, man became accustomed to associate with the feeling of being admired for his intelligence, his courage, and so on, a very strong sense of pleasure; so that, quite apart from utility, whenever the first feeling occurred, the second followed out of habit. Man takes particular pleasure in admiration of his courage, his mind, his strength, his prowess, for its own sake: for this reason, man is particularly vain.

Men accordingly aspire to be distinguished for acts or achievements of intelligence, courage, and spirit (often, too, from the false semblance of these), to gain admiration, and not only the admiration of those whose opinion of them is useful but the admiration of many whose opinion of them is of no use at all. For they know that, as we have already said, a strong sense of pleasure arises from all admiration, and a strong sense of displeasure from all contempt.

The fact that we love admiration not solely on account of its utility, but also by itself, is what makes our striving for admiration and distinction so various. Admiration can be of actual use to us only in individual cases and on the part of individuals; taken by itself, however, it can come to us from countless people. For example, a writer who enjoys admiration for its own sake will strive for the admiration of a whole nation, or various nations, or all his contemporaries (ambition) or, in anticipation, strive for the admiration of coming generations (obsession with fame). The greater the admiration, the greater the sense of pleasure. If on the other hand he enjoys admiration for its utility, he will seek to distinguish himself by writing only in the particular cases useful to him, and only in the eyes of the particular people useful to him, and only until he has achieved benefits such as a comfortable position. His striving for distinction and admiration is limited, whereas the striving of the person who enjoys admiration by itself is unlimited.

Similarly, if, among the many situations in which we displease or are somehow despised and scorned, we were pained only by those that made us fear some disadvantage from this contempt, we would have to suffer only in a few cases and on account of a few persons. As it is, since contempt itself is painful to us, we suffer from it in the many situations in which we displease in general or are disdained, despised, and scorned.

The vain person, as we said at the beginning of this chapter, does not want solely to please or be admired for some quality: he also wants to be envied. It is obvious that this pleasure in arousing envy does not arise from the fact that envy is originally felt as pleasurable on account of its useful consequences, and only then as pleasurable by itself. For the person who is envied has to expect evil rather than good consequences. Instead, the satisfaction in arousing envy is to be explained in the following way.

First, There are two sorts of envy: envy out of self-interest and envy out of vanity.

Envy out of self-interest is concerned with the utility that the envied person gets from qualities of external possessions (e.g., a fine home) or of body (e.g., health) or of mind (e.g., intelligence). Others are often envious when someone pleases and is admired, on account of the utility that person gets from pleasing or being admired (e.g., professional envy).

When the person who is envied enjoys this envy, it is because the envy brings to mind clearly the value of the envied quality (e.g., his health).

Envy out of vanity has to do not with the utility enjoyed by the envied person but rather with the satisfaction of his vanity; and so with the fact that he pleases or is admired, or with the quality on account of which he pleases or is admired (e.g., cleverness or beauty).

When the envied person enjoys this envy, it is because the envy brings to mind how much he pleases or is admired, how much he is distinguished from others. For example, a woman who is admired by men for her beauty will feel the envy of other women as pleasurable, because this envy shows her particularly clearly how much she is distinguished from the others.

All admiration presupposes the comparison of something relatively great with something relatively small. It is from the perception of what is great in contrast with what is small that the feeling called admiration arises. Thus, the person who is enjoying being admired (whether this is for the sake of utility, or by itself) will turn his attention about and simultaneously enjoy the presence of the condition that enables him to be admired, that is, to be distinguished from others as more handsome, more popular, or greater as a writer or orator. The fact that others have fallen behind him cannot, as we have said, be made clearer to him than through their envy; this is why being admired is a very pleasant feeling. (Certainly, envious persons usually hide their envy, partly because it is regarded as immoral and partly because they do not want to admit that they have fallen behind anyone.) Envy out of vanity thus presupposes three persons, namely, the envious person, that is, the one who is envious because another person pleases or is admired more than himself; the envied person; and the person or persons who prefer the one above the other.

We have seen that pleasing and being admired is felt as pleasant at first for its useful consequences and later owing to acquired habit; that women aspire very specifically to be admired for their beauty, and men for their physical or intellectual strength; we saw further that the person who is admired must be distinguished from others and that, therefore, whoever can be admired enjoys being distinguished from others and enjoys especially the clearest sign of this distinction, namely, the envy of others.

The question now is whether vanity is innate or acquired afresh with each generation. Its innateness could be explained in the following way: since our ancestors were vain for countless generations—for even in the most ancient tribes, the individual must often have had to take the opinion of others into account, as we have said, at first out of utility but later by itself, owing to acquired habit—this habit of taking account of the opinion of others by itself, of striving for distinction and feeling pain at being disregarded, has become innate as an instinct in later generations. That this is possible, that the habits of ancestors, if they are maintained across many generations, can appear in their descendants as hereditary instinct, admits of no doubt. When, for example, our young sheep dogs are taken out for the first time, an innate instinct encourages them to run all around the flock. But this running around was not always the instinct of their race: rather, it was inculcated into their ancestors by shepherds (one can find other examples in Darwin's *Variation of Animals and Plants under Domestication*).[21] On the other hand, it is also possible that such an inheritance has not yet occurred in the case of vanity, and that each generation undergoes afresh from childhood the experience that pleasing and being admired bring advantages, while displeasing and being despised bring disadvantages, so that, owing to acquired habit, the first situation is felt as pleasant apart from its utility, and the second as disagreeable apart from its harmfulness. The author has not been able to arrive at a definite opinion on this point.

Let us consider now the extent to which people ordinarily condemn vanity.

What they condemn most is vanity in the narrower sense (i.e., striving to please, to be admired and envied now). Ambition (i.e., striving to acquire in the future those things that arouse envy and admiration) is condemned less, and the sense of honor (i.e., the fear of dishonor) is praised.

The reasons why vanity in the narrower sense is condemned are moral, eudemonistic, and intellectual.

(1) *The moral reason.* To be admired one must distinguish oneself above others, as we have said, and the envy of others is pleasant because it is the clearest sign that one has in fact distinguished oneself above them. The envied person is himself envious, that is, of those who are distinguished above him and more admired than him. Such envy is a tormenting sensation; one hates those who arouse it and, to get rid of it, one destroys wherever possible the qualities that arouse this envy. For example, the woman who is less beautiful would like to scratch the beauty from the face of the one who is more beautiful; inferior writers, painters, orators, and professors would like to do away with superior ones.

The vain person is thus envious and, while happy to be envied himself, he hates and harms others—feelings and actions that are directly opposed to what people usually regard as praiseworthy, namely, love of one's neighbor.

Moreover, the vain person does not present himself to others as he is; he hides everything that could inspire a bad opinion of him and affects whatever can inspire a good opinion.

(2) *The eudemonistic reason.* The vain person experiences many sensations of displeasure and few of pleasure. For he does not always please when he wants to please, and in any case, the pleasure taken in pleasing is much less than the pain suffered in displeasing. The majority fail in their attempts to distinguish themselves and excite admiration, whether because their own beauty or achievements fall well behind the beauty and achievements of others or because feeble human judgment prefers the worse to the better. These failures produce a deep discon-

tent: anyone who seeks admiration and finds in its place only indifference or contempt feels pain, and indeed a pain much greater than the pleasure of the person who receives admiration. Finally, the admired person himself is never so exclusively admired that he does not run into others who are even more admired, because even more beautiful, more adroit, more gifted than he. He envies these people, just as he himself is envied by others. His feeling of envy is more painful to him, however, than his provoking of envy is pleasant to him.

Thus, we do not always please, we seldom arouse admiration, and we often feel envy. In contrast—and this is exceptional—the person who pleases everyone, always attracts admiration, and is so prominent that many envy him but who himself never has occasion for envy, such a person loses his joy in pleasing, in being admired and envied, out of habit.

It is because vanity by its nature generates displeasure that the moralists have condemned it and advised us not to be vain. They say, "Whether you please or not, whether you are distinguished from others or not, is something that should concern you solely in the relatively few cases where displeasing or not being distinguished is harmful to you. When you feel dissatisfaction at displeasing or not being distinguished and admired, and then are envious of those who are more admired than you, if you do not expect any harm from this lack of distinction or any utility from its opposite, it is irrational that you should sacrifice your comfort, your well-being and your fortune to gain distinction, and also blameworthy, especially bearing in mind the misanthropic feeling of envy."

Since blaming makes sense only on the assumption that human nature contains the power to change what is blamed, this blame makes no sense.

Thus, even the moralists concede that people must often strive for distinction on account of its utility; a woman who wants to marry must not displease but rather please some man more than other women do; a worker who wants to be promoted must distinguish himself over other workers. But where someone has often associated a feeling of pleasure with the feeling of being distinguished over others for beauty or skill, because of the utility of being distinguished, and associated a feeling of displeasure with the feeling of seeing others distinguished as superior to him, because of the disadvantages of inferiority, this person cannot help it afterward if, whenever one of these feelings occurs, such as the feeling of inferiority, the other one, the feeling of displeasure, occurs as well (quite apart from utility). Thus, a woman feels pain each time she pleases less than another woman. This pain occurs involuntarily, and the reflection that it is irrational to feel pain over inferiority, even in situations where no disadvantage is expected from it, cannot prevent the feeling from occurring; nor too can reflection do much about this feeling of pain once it is occurring. One may remark in particular that, whenever we feel pain over being inferior to others because that is a disadvantage, the acquired habit of feeling pain over being inferior simply by itself is reinforced. It is for this reason that, as long as we give the first feeling of pain the opportunity to occur, that is, as long as we live together with others, the second feeling of pain will be inevitable.

So we cannot help feeling envy toward those who are distinguished as superior to us, and yet this feeling can hardly be condemned. For anyone who is condemned because he feels pain over displeasing, or envies those who are superior to him, may certainly form a resolution not to worry about displeasing, or not to feel envy in the future; such a resolution, however, is useless, since, given that these feelings are involuntary, he will suffer the next time he displeases, despite his resolution, and will envy those who are superior to him.

There is just one way for people to avoid the pain of displeasing or of seeing others distinguished as superior to them, and that is for them to go alone into the forests and avoid any *occasion* for suffering from the opinion of others. As soon as people live together, each must often strive to be distinguished as superior on account of his utility, and later, as we have said, he cannot prevent himself from feeling superiority as pleasant by itself and inferiority as unpleasant by itself, by reason of habit.

If, therefore, people, although acknowledging that vanity brings them many pains and few pleasures, cannot remove it from their minds, if they are not capable of becoming indifferent to the opinion of others taken by itself and so becoming indifferent to displeasing and not being distinguished or admired, then it is rational for them to take account of the fact that they cannot eliminate vanity from their behavior, except at the cost of their well-being. Anyone who, for example, would displease, or at least not be considered as dressing well, if he did not wear tight and uncomfortable clothing, is acting rationally in choosing such clothes if his pain in displeasing or not being distinguished outweighs his physical comfort, that is, if he prefers being distinguished, even if that involves physical suffering, to a physical comfort associated with a lack of distinction. The same applies to a splendid but uncomfortable home, position, or manner. It is quite rational if anyone in determining his behavior takes account of the degree to which he is sensitive to a lack of distinction, and if this is great, imposes constraints on his comfort, well-being, and health; or if it is weak, does the opposite. In the latter case, he will no longer dress himself uncomfortably, or live in an uncomfortable home, or perform extraordinary and admirable actions or works for the sake of distinction, beyond the point where this involves any sacrifice of his fortune, comfort, and well-being.

I repeat: if anyone could strip himself of his vanity, it would be rational to do so. For even if vanity sometimes brings him feelings of pleasure, that is, when he pleases or is admired and envied, it far more often brings him strong feelings of displeasure, that is, when he displeases, encounters indifference instead of admiration, or feels envy instead of exciting envy. However, as he cannot strip himself of his vanity, he is acting rationally when he avoids displeasing, meeting with indifference in others, or feeling envy himself, even sometimes at the cost of his comfort and well-being. This is how people act instinctively, and hence their behavior is not as irrational as the moralists tend to assume: on the contrary, it is the best among possible behaviors.

(3) *The intellectual reason.* Insofar as he is vain, man is not objective: he is interested in nature, art, philosophy, and science not for their own sake, but because he wants to please and gain the admiration of others through knowledge of them. This lack of commitment means that he does not study these subjects thoroughly or gain the intellectual pleasure that a purely objective interest in such subjects provides.

Since vanity is regarded as blameworthy for the reasons indicated—that is, (1) because it makes a person hostile to those who are superior to him and incites him to hypocrisy; (2) because it gives him a number of painful feelings when he suffers from not pleasing, etc.; and (3) because the vain person is not objective—we do not admit our vanity, but give quite different reasons for the many actions we carry out to please and to be admired, and for the many discomforts and sacrifices we accept for the same reasons. Many people expressly emphasize that they are not vain: they are vain of their lack of vanity.

The reasons why ambition is condemned are, similarly:

(1) *A moral reason.* The end for whose sake the ambitious person gathers riches, conquers countries, or writes books is to be distinguished over others, to arouse envy and admiration. No doubt this end does not appear as clearly with the ambitious person as with the vain person: the vain person wants to please and be admired and envied now, and this offensive intention is immediately apparent to others; in contrast, the ambitious person does not want to be admired now: he first sets out to acquire the advantages that excite envy and admiration, and hence, all that appears immediately is a great exertion of intellectual and physical forces, which is ordinarily also useful to the community. This activity conceals his offensive intention: here the means justify the end, so to speak. Thus the ambitious person appears less blameworthy than the vain person, although the end he pursues is identical.

(2) *The eudemonistic reason.* Ambition, although it is ordinarily useful to the community, provides for the ambitious person himself only a laborious activity, without ever affording him enjoyment. First of all, he must accomplish achievements that are more important, intelligent, or artistically beautiful than the achievements of others. If he actually succeeds in some such achievement,

he nevertheless does not feel satisfied, but is immediately plotting to surpass those who are still ahead of him. Hence, he begins his laborious activity again, and so forth. The moralist calls to him, "Enjoy the present, instead of chasing after an honor that you are as unlikely to enjoy as the miser is to enjoy the money piled up before him."

The sufferings of the ambitious person are thus different from those of the vain person: as we have said, the vain person wants to please and be admired now and suffers if he does not succeed. The ambitious person, in contrast, does not want to be admired now: his suffering consists in the hard labor by which he strives all the time to obtain the things that excite admiration (riches, conquests, productions).

Despite the ambitious person's incessant and yet aimless activity, it is unreasonable to condemn him for it. For, if this condemnation takes effect and the ambitious person ceases his labors, he will fall victim to a much greater evil—boredom.

There are, in fact, only two sorts of human activity: an activity that has the well-being of the agent as its ultimate end, and an activity that has the well-being of others as its ultimate end. The first divides into purely intellectual activity (that is, an objective concern for nature, art, philosophy, and science) and activity for the satisfaction of drives (the drive for self-preservation, the sexual drive, and vanity). Of these three activities, that is, activity for the satisfaction of drives, purely intellectual activity, and activity for the sake of others, the last two are rare and weak.

When someone who is active out of ambition gives up this activity, he can devote himself either to an activity of the same sort or to one of the other two sorts: he can either seek the satisfaction of his needs for food, clothing, and housing (the drive for self-preservation) and for reproduction, or engage in objective (scientific or artistic) activities, or care for others for their own sake. We will see, however, that for most people who give up ambition, none of these activities provides an occupation sufficient to prevent boredom.

The person who has rationally given up ambition will not have to look after needs for nourishment, etc., since he has already provided for them. Otherwise he would not have devoted himself to ambition: anyone who suffers from a lack of these primary needs thinks solely of their satisfaction, not of the satisfaction of his ambition. Only the well-fed person is ambitious. Hence, for those who cease to work out of ambition, concern for primary needs cannot provide an occupation.

Furthermore, a purely objective concern with art and science cannot give rise to a true occupation for most people. For the intellect was not originally designed for purely objective knowledge: it was developed in the struggle for existence. That is, the apes, ape-men, or men-apes who survived and repro-duced themselves were those who, thanks to their greater intelligence, were more capable of escaping from their enemies, gaining nourishment, and over-coming their rivals. Thus, what emerges from the history of the intellectual faculties is that our intellectual strength exists first of all for the satisfaction of our instincts and not for purely objective knowledge of the true and the good. Accordingly, human beings use their intellect to provide satisfaction for their instincts: they think in order to acquire provisions, wives, reputation, and riches; they take an interest in art and science usually to obtain admiration, only exceptionally and temporarily with objective aims. A capacity for lasting concern with these for their own sake requires an extraordinary and excessive formation of the intellect: that is, so-called genius. Yet even the genius would never complete a single work in all its parts unless a desire for fame maintained the fire of his activity. A painter, for example, seized by the beauty of a land-scape, can certainly set out to present it as a picture; but from the conception and plan of genius up to the execution of a masterpiece in its various parts there is such a long and laborious route to be covered that the greatest genius would be disabled if this labor had to gain its energy from love of the work alone. The same is true of all artistic, scientific, and philosophical works. If ambition were to disappear, even geniuses—let alone ordinary beings with-out genius—would have little chance of finding in art and science an activity sufficient to drive away their boredom.

In the end, non-egoistic, unselfish activity is very rare. We are usually of ser-vice to others so that they will be of service to us in turn: the drive to care for others for their own sake is weak. It is still less part of human nature (as it usu-ally exists) to make selfless behavior an occupation that fills up the hours of one's day. One cannot even increase the number of one's selfless actions at will. For since selfless behavior rests on selfless feelings, and since these selfless feel-ings (compassion, benevolence) are involuntary, anyone can act in an selfless manner only when he has a selfless feeling, which is rare, as we have said. Thus, anyone who, following a selfless impulse, is active for others for their own sake will soon cease this activity unless his non-egoistic instinct is extraordinarily strong: the motivation for the activity will soon be lost.

I repeat: if those who are now active out of ambition give up this activity, no other human activities will provide them with an occupation. They have already attended to their needs for nourishment, clothing etc.; apart from that, it is a long way from ordinary human nature to make an occupation out of purely objective or selfless activity. But other activities do not exist. These people therefore fall victim to boredom, which is a greater evil than even the hardest labor. In fact, we see most of those who have retired from business and are left only with pastimes suffering from this evil. For that reason, those who work to attain great riches, brilliant positions, and the like should not be encouraged to give up their work for the sake of happiness, even if it is very demanding, for they would fall victim to boredom.

(3) *The intellectual reason.* The ambitious person occupies himself with science and art not for their own sake, but because he wants to gain the admiration of others through his achievements. Hence, the following distinction can be made between ambition and vanity: We call someone vain when he strives to excite admiration by the acquaintances he already possesses or the achievements he has already accomplished. On the other hand, we call someone ambitious when he sets out to acquire admirable acquaintances or to accomplish admirable achievements. Nevertheless, we demand that the person who occupies himself with art and science should have a total and disinterested commitment to them, as we have already said.

The ambitious person, although criticized for his lack of objectivity and his irrationality, is ordinarily condemned less than the vain person, because his activities disguise his offensive intentions and because they are commonly useful. For this reason, many admit that they are ambitious—that they have the will and the capacity to surpass others. Most ambitious people no doubt say they have no ambition, to suggest that they take an interest in, for example, art or science for its own sake, or that they work for others for their own sake.

Finally, the sense of honor is praised, although it provides only feelings of displeasure and is not morally praiseworthy.

It arouses feelings of displeasure in us first whenever we are disdained, despised, or scorned, and second when, in order to escape this contempt, we impose constraints on our opinions or our well-being or even sacrifice even our life (e.g., in order not to be seen as a coward). If we did not have this sense of honor, contempt by itself would arouse no sense of displeasure in us, and we would be bothered by it only in cases where we expected a disadvantage from it; whereas as it is contempt does bother us by itself, as we have said, and hence does so whenever we are despised at all.

It is rational to use force against one's desires in order to escape contempt or disdain where this constraint is less painful to one than contempt. For instance, the person for whom a life of shame is more unbearable than death will act rationally in taking his life when contempt falls upon him. On the other hand, the person for whom death is more unbearable than a life of shame will act rationally in remaining alive when contempt falls upon him: this is a matter of taste. The same applies, as we have seen, to the positive aspect of vanity. It is rational to impose constraints on one's other inclinations for the sake of admiration, that is, in order to be regarded as especially courageous, wise, or good, when the pain of this constraint is less than the pleasure received from admiration. It is just as rational sometimes to impose constraints on one's inclinations on account of contempt, that is, in order not to be regarded as especially cowardly or ignorant. The only difference is that whereas the constraint imposed out of vanity is supposed to lead to a positive pleasure, namely, the pleasure of being admired, the constraint imposed on account of the sense of honor results in the absence of a pain, namely, the pain of being despised.

Further, the fact that the sense of honor is not morally praiseworthy is due to the essential nature of this feeling. Only actions performed for the sake of others are counted as morally good. However, actions arising from the sense of honor are performed not for the sake of others but for one's own sake. For instance, the person who is brave in order not to be taken as a coward is, given his motives, acting for himself and not for others. The same conclusion emerges from the following: someone can have a very strong sense of honor and yet be very egoistic. For instance, someone who firmly believes that a cruel action he wants to commit will never be known by anyone will not be held back from committing such an action by even the strongest sense of honor, that is, by the strongest pain resulting from the contempt of others.

Being good and having a sense of honor are thus different things. Being good means having non-egoistic feelings and acting accordingly, while having a sense of honor means feeling pain at being despised and acting accordingly. The fact that the sense of honor is nevertheless commonly praised is to be explained in the following way. In the first place, the sense of honor, in contrast with vanity, is not morally blameworthy. For whereas the vain person who wants to distinguish himself is envious of those who are superior to him and happy when he excites envy, nobody wants to distinguish himself from a sense of honor: for example, the soldier who has a sense of honor does not want to be regarded as braver than his comrades but only as no less brave; the citizen who has a sense of honor does not want to be regarded as better, but only as no worse than other citizens of his nation or class. One does not want a particularly good opinion or admiration (in which only a few people can share, and which thus creates envy, hate, and hostility) but only an opinion that is not particularly bad; one does not want to be despised—which can happen to many at the same time (for example, all the soldiers of a company) and so generates no hostile rivalry between individuals.

Actions out of a sense of honor are therefore not morally blameworthy and, if they are not morally praiseworthy either, since their motivation is egoistic, they are at any rate useful, especially for the preservation of the state, recalling that every civil community continues to exist only through the fear of punishment. If the power of the state were to disappear, and punishment with it, the stronger would immediately seize the property of the weaker, and even take their lives if that were to their advantage: the war of all against all would be inevitable. But within punishment itself, we must still distinguish between the actual suffering it inflicts (e.g., imprisonment) and the shame that falls upon the person punished as a thief, forger, or robber. The first suffering is temporary, whereas the sense of dishonor is a lasting torment, often throughout an entire lifetime. Hence, it is the fear of this dishonor, rather than the actual suffering inflicted by punishment, that restrains the citizens of a state. So much more effective is this fear that without it, even draconian legislation could hardly maintain peace within a state.

In addition, the sense of honor prevents the soldier from being a coward and the official from being negligent, and even for the educator the fear of dishonor is an important resource.

Owing to this utility, the sense of honor is counted among praiseworthy things.

Thus, we praise the fear of dishonor, that is, the fear of being regarded as more cowardly, morally bad, ignorant, or negligent than other members of the same state or occupation. We praise the ambitious person's desire to achieve accomplishments through which he will not only not be inferior to others but will come to the fore among them as particularly courageous, good, popular, or wise, when we are looking at the advantages produced by his activity, and we condemn it when we are looking at his (seeming) irrationality in regard to himself and at his offensive intention (to excite admiration and envy). If the ambitious person takes an interest in science and art, we condemn his lack of objectivity. The person who is vain in the narrower sense wants to please or be admired and envied as particularly courageous, good, or intelligent now; his intention emerges immediately instead of being hidden by his activity, as with the ambitious person. And so it is strongly condemned, that is, (1) because in order to attain his end he presents himself as other than he is; (2) because his behavior encourages rivalry, envy, hate, and hostility; 3) because it gives him many unpleasant feelings and few pleasant feelings (since he often displeases, etc.); and (4) because he is not objective.

We pass now to the situations and feelings which are entirely or partly based upon vanity.

(1) *Two states of illusion.* The distinction between the non-egoist as good and the egoist as bad is, as we saw, not as old as the human race, but is the product of a later cultural stage. However, once this distinction has been made, it is transformed in the mind of those who accept it into a moral principle that they

apply to human character—praising it when it is non-egoistic and condemning it when it is egoistic at the expense of others. Since this distinction has penetrated our every pore, so to speak, since our childhood, the image of a selfless individual exists in our mind as a sacred authority or exemplary model. Everyone wants to seem to match this exemplary model so that his behavior will appear praiseworthy to other people who, as he knows, carry this same exemplary model within themselves.

One recalls, first of all, the fact that the non-egoistic drive is very weak in human beings and the egoistic drive very strong. Their motto is, as Schopenhauer remarks, "Everything for me and nothing for the others."[22] Hence, they always strive to possess what belongs to others and feel malevolence, envy, and hate toward others. That these drives cannot readily be satisfied within a civil community (because of punishment and the shame associated with it) we have already said several times. However, the consequence of the fact that people find non-egoism good and egoism bad is that, far from openly satisfying this egoistic drive, we never let it be seen but conceal it and affect non-egoistic feelings in its place. From this results an encompassing state of illusion: everyone acts as if they were highly interested in the well-being of others, when in fact they are highly interested only in their own well-being.

The reason why we want to appear similar to the exemplary model present in the minds of others, and thus praiseworthy, is in part our personal interest: we want to inspire their trust through being non-egoistic; and in part our vanity: it is pleasant to us by itself to be taken as good, unpleasant by itself to be taken as bad.

This hypocrisy, owing to which we disguise forbidden feelings such as greed, envy, and hate, and affect the feelings considered good, such as courage, honesty, and benevolence, is bad insofar as that it undermines people's trust in one another. Yet it is inevitable. Its elimination would be imaginable, on the one hand, if only people presented themselves as they are, in which case most of them would show their teeth to one another, for malevolence, greed, and envy are strong among them. To make use of a metaphor, the peaceable words that two people exchange are, so to speak, only the peaceably behaving sentinels of the armies of hostile feelings encamped in their hearts. Thus, if people did present themselves as they are, they could never associate with one another. On the other hand, this hypocrisy would be eliminated if only people were as they present themselves, that is, full of benevolence and thus without malevolence, envy, and hate. That is, however, not within their power. For since their non-egoistic drive is weak and their egoistic drive strong, they have many egoistic impulses and few non-egoistic impulses.

Thus, if people want to associate with one another, they must not present themselves to one another as they are; and yet they do not have the capacity to be as they present themselves. In consequence, they must present themselves as what they are not.

The fact that people conceal their egoism—in part out of personal interest in order to inspire trust, in part out of vanity in order not to be taken as bad, and in part because if they openly displayed their egoism, no association between them would be possible—accounts for the appeal of many writings that bring it to light. It is interesting to recognize human nature as it actually is, in contrast with its pretence—a theme whose subtle treatment is especially great among the French, such as La Rochefoucauld, Saint Réal, Chamfort and others, and, among the Germans, Schopenhauer. The novels of Lesage are also interesting, mainly for their recognition of the difference between the appearance and the reality of human nature. His stories are mostly illustrations of moral maxims, and so do not have as much artistic value as, for example, the novels of Goethe and Walter Scott. Similarly, the interest we take in Shakespeare's characters is based, at least in part, on the fact that in them, we see people as they truly are in their feelings, whereas life shows us only their pretended feelings. For instance, the Gonerils of real life usually conceal the hardness of their hearts in order not to be denounced as bad and instead affect benevolent impulses, such as gratitude.

The conviction that the bottom of the human heart is full of selfishness and envy is often labeled with the expression "despair of humanity."

In addition to this moral state of illusion, I draw attention to an intellectual state of illusion.

We said earlier that the original function of our faculty of knowledge is to provide us with nourishment, women, and in general fodder for the satisfaction of our instincts, whereas purely objective knowledge of the true and good presupposes an extraordinary intellect, a genius. We also saw that even the genius can be kept at the hard labor required for the completion of any work only by external reasons such as ambition and the desire for fame. It is even more certain that the great number of those who produce scientific, philosophical, and artistic works, while not possessing genius, work much less out of love of their subject than out of love of their own fame.

Similarly, a passive absorption and enjoyment of nature, art, and philosophy presupposes gifts and culture much higher than those of ordinary people (who are seriously occupied only with earning their bread). Most people visit beautiful landscapes only to relax, to make acquaintances of whom they can boast back home, and to have seen as much as or more than others, and the person who looks at a beautiful landscape is thinking of the landscape itself only for a few moments; his thoughts soon turn away and become occupied with everyday concerns. Even the reading of the classics is felt by most not as a pleasure, but as a tedious labor that they try to get over and done with. They read them to know as much "as any educated person has to know" if he does not want to be despised. This lack of objectivity is cultivated as much as possible by our schools (i.e., by the torture chambers in which teachers without spirit, whose heads are stuffed full with scattered knowledge, spoil everything of the mind for us). The pupil learns either from fear of punishment or in the hope of surpassing others, and so he becomes used not to gaining any knowledge with objective aims.

Despite this, people do not ordinarily admit that they produce works out of ambition or a desire for fame and that their absorption in or experience of nature, art, and philosophy usually provides no pleasure, but takes place for external reasons. They want to be taken as possessing the higher intellectuality required for understanding and enjoying these subjects. In this way, a second illusion arises: out of vanity, people act as if they are taking an interest in nature, art, and philosophy with objective motives, when in fact they do so for reasons that are not objective. They commonly act in the same way toward themselves: for it is not only in the estimation of the world but also in their own estimation that they want to appear to dominate others intellectually, or at least not to fall behind them. For this reason, most people are not at all aware of what is truly boring or interesting, ugly or beautiful for them.

The topic of illusion is not exhausted with the moral illusion in virtue of which one presents oneself as more benevolent than one is or with the intellectual illusion in virtue of which one presents oneself as more intellectual than one is; rather, it is inexhaustible. Nevertheless, we shall now leave it to itself and pass on to:

(2) *Feelings closely related to vanity.* Malicious pleasure [*Schadenfreude*] is usually explained by the association of ideas, on the model of Lucretius. When one sees, for example, a boat shipwrecked on the sea, one feels satisfaction at the thought of one's own safety.[23] The misfortune of others reminds us that we are not unfortunate. There exists, however, a second kind of malicious pleasure, in which the suffering of others pleases us not because it reminds us of our own good fortune, but because it gives us a feeling of superiority over the victim (being distinguished over him). When, for example, one among a number of riders falls from his horse, the malicious pleasure of the others consists in enjoying either their own good fortune or their superiority over him (as more skilful riders). This second kind of malicious pleasure, based on vanity, is commonly much more intense than the first kind, and the enjoyment it provides tends to be expressed as ridicule of the victim: a case of "adding insult to injury."[24]

The examples just given presuppose that the person who feels malicious pleasure is better off than the victim. Often, however, they are just as badly off. The fallen rider will feel malicious pleasure if another rider also falls off. The fact that this other stayed in the saddle was painful to him—either because that made him feel the discomfort of his own situation particularly keenly or because he felt his inferiority to the others (as a less skillful rider). He is freed from both of these feelings of displeasure as soon as the other also falls. Hence, the *socios habuisse malorum*.[25]

The sweetness of revenge is explained on the same model. That is: if someone has inflicted suffering on us, he thereby proves his strength and his superiority over us. If we are in a position to inflict a similar or, if possible, an even greater suffering on him, we refute the proof of his superiority over us and show that we are superior or at least equal to him. (Schopenhauer gives the same explanation.[26]) The satisfaction felt in annoying someone in return has the same origin.

The feeling of justice must not be confused with the desire for vengeance.[27] In virtue of this feeling, we demand that the person who has acted badly should undergo suffering as a retribution—whether his wickedness has been directed against us or against others: it is right that punishment should fall on him (cf. chapter 4). In contrast, we revenge ourselves only on those who have harmed us or those close to us, and what drives us to this is not the feeling of justice but, as we have already said, the desire to make our strength and our superiority felt. The origin of the desire for vengeance is vanity (the satisfaction of distinguishing oneself, of showing oneself superior to anyone who has tried to demonstrate his superiority over one). The origin of the feeling of justice is the habit in virtue of which, from our childhood on, we consider crime and punishment as two things that rightly belong together. In consequence of our education, we hold the feeling of justice to be praiseworthy and the desire for vengeance to be blameworthy. (With the Greeks, the desire for vengeance was counted as praiseworthy). Yet despite our education, although we find the desire for vengeance blameworthy, we cannot help sympathizing with the person who takes revenge: he is not a weakling, he lets nobody impose on him, we would do the same thing, and so forth.

We are happy to increase the intensity of vengeance by *cruelty*. For every torment we inflict on our enemy is evidence of our power over him. Certainly, many are cruel toward people who have never done them any harm. This cruelty also rests in part on the desire to establish one's own superiority (to this extent, there is no satisfaction in being cruel to children, old people, or invalids, since the sense of superiority to them is already complete without that); and it also rests in part on the nervous emotions that agree with the blunted nerves of the cruel person. It is for this reason too that the nervous emotion called voluptuousness is often associated with cruelty.

Jealousy arises when someone prefers another person to us, and this rejection is painful to us either because of some disadvantage or by itself.

Pride arises in the following way. Someone compares his own qualities or achievements with the qualities or achievements of others, finds his own to be superior, and now associates the idea of a superior person, distinguished above others, with the idea of himself, for example, as a writer, without caring any more about the opinion of the world; rather, in his awareness of being superior, the opinion of others is a matter of indifference to him. If he expresses this awareness of his merits through his behavior, he is called proud. (If he does not express it through his behavior, he is called modest; if his opinion of himself is greater than his actual merits, and this is expressed in his behavior, he is called presumptuous.) When the proud person, such as the proud writer, does not get appropriate recognition from his contemporaries, he is consoled by the thought that it will come to him after his death: he associates with the idea of himself as a writer the idea of an admired writer, and indeed one who is admired for all time.

(3) *Details.* When a girl is seduced, that is, surrenders to a man without his offering her marriage in return, other women have an interest in expelling this girl from their society. For if they did not do so, every girl would be seduced and men would only rarely marry—only rarely undertake the lifelong care of a woman and children. Partly for the sake of this care, and partly because the position of woman would lose respect with the abolition of marriage, a rigorous observation is imposed on women, so that they exclude the unchaste girls who have acted against this interest and cast as much shame as possible on them.

The seducer, on the other hand, incurs condemnation because he has exposed the seduced girl to shame, but does not incur shame for his own having sexual relations outside marriage. For the male sex has no interest in the chastity of its members (i.e., their having sexual relations only within marriage) and therefore does not label men as unchaste.

Certainly in many places (e.g., in Paris) a distinction is made between the chastity of women and of girls. Women allow one another lovers. For once marriage has been entered into, it is usually not dissolved, despite adultery. (In Catholic countries it is completely indissoluble.) In contrast, girls are allowed no lovers, for otherwise no marriage at all would be entered into. Indeed, out of fear that the unchastity of women might be passed on to girls, so that the number of marriages would be reduced, girls are watched over all the more strictly where the unchastity of women is greatest (as is the case in France).

In places where sexual relations are forbidden for women, the idea of what is shameful and dishonorable is associated with the idea of the woman who has a lover. When a woman does have the desire to take a lover, she is afraid that he too might associate these two ideas with each other: she is afraid of being despised if she gives herself. Hence, she seems to decide on this step only with the greatest difficulty: she is not easy, "she is not like the others"; in short, she wants to be what is called wicked and yet seem to be what is called virtuous. Sometimes she will resist a timid admirer for a long time. For his timidity indicates that he, like her, considers infidelity to be something important, something which a woman should really not commit and which it is shameful to commit. The bold admirer, on the other hand, seems not to place much importance on infidelity, and so the woman who is unfaithful with him is not afraid of being despised by him: she therefore gives herself more readily.

Incidentally, the strength of the sexual instinct comes from the fact that, throughout countless generations, the animals and human beings who left the most descendants were those whose sexual instinct was strongest. These descendants then inherited the strength of this instinct, and so on in turn.

Enjoyment of so-called gossip or pulling people to pieces consists in seeking out every discernible fault of a person in order to enjoy a sense of superiority by displaying these faults clearly to oneself and to others.

If the person gossiped about is the successful rival of the gossiping individual, the enjoyment of degrading him in words relieves the pain of seeing his superiority to oneself in reality.

Gossip is thus a kind of vanity and is the necessary pastime of all those who, since they have no intellectual interests (like the majority of even educated people), are bored in their hours of leisure.

The female sex gossips more than the male sex, partly because their intellectual interests are much narrower (in consequence of their position and education) and partly because women are rivals among themselves to a much greater degree than men.

A girl who suits wearing a mourning dress might kill a relative from time to time: this is a hyperbole. But: a girl who suits wearing a mourning dress may rejoice in the death of a relative for that reason: this is not a hyperbole.

Dueling is commonly argued against in the following way: when someone has offended you (i.e., has expressed his disdain or contempt to you by words, behavior, or expression) it is irrational to choose to fight a duel to avenge the offense. For if you are killed—what has your revenge consisted in?

The reply to this is: no offended person thinks that it is rational to fight a duel, by itself. On the contrary, he understands that it is irrational to seek to satisfy one's desire for vengeance in a combat that gives the offender just as many chances as himself. But, if he does not fight a duel, the world will despise him: custom labels as cowardly anyone who refuses to fight after having been offended. Anyone to whom the thought of being regarded as a coward is more painful than death or a mortal wound will be rationally motivated to fight by an offence.

Thus, dueling cannot be abolished by exposing its irrationality in the way just indicated. Everyone already recognizes this irrationality. Instead, it would have to be brought about that those who do not fight a duel are not despised. This, however, could come about only if the persons who *set the tone* did not choose to fight a duel in response to an offence. For what they do is regarded not as despicable but as acceptable: they are more powerful than the custom they clash with, and so the custom perishes in consequence; whereas the ordinary person is weaker than the custom and, in any clash with this custom, he is the one who perishes.

Thus, if the custom of despising the person who does not fight a duel in response to an offence disappears, then dueling will also disappear.

The state in any case favors dueling. For what matters to it is that its citizens have a strong sense of honor.* The duel shows this sense of honor (fear of being regarded as a coward).

    ❦

Being admired (fame, riches, respect) appears to us such a great happiness that we never envy those who are poor and not respected, even if they are happy; indeed, we are not even capable of appreciating their happiness, because it lies outside the desires that occupy us daily and hourly. We do not envy happiness but the appearance of happiness.

    ❦

When we reject an aspiring lover, we feel our superiority over him very clearly, for we do not allow him any power over us; we dominate without being dominated.

But the rejected person now has a redoubled interest in gaining possession of the object of his love. For now he has to obtain satisfaction not only for his

---

* See above, pp. 140–41.

love, but in addition for his vanity, which has perhaps been wounded by preference given to another. He therefore strives for possession with redoubled zeal
(this familiar fact, that jealousy increases love, is often cleverly used, especially by women) but without understanding that he desires more now than before out of vanity: he does not sense this reason for his fervent striving, only
the fervent striving itself, and so the object so ardently desired now appears
to him even more attractive, gracious, and beautiful than before—as more
desirable for its own sake than before. He deceives himself about the true reason for the desire that has become so strong since his rejection: he takes the
personal advantages of the woman as this reason, when his vanity is the real
reason.

If in the end he achieves possession, the woman immediately loses in his
eyes the charms he had attributed to her as long as his desire was increased by
rejection; she no longer appears to him as attractive or gracious or beautiful:
he is disillusioned.

To this disillusion resting on vanity are often added two more disillusions:

(1) Before possession, we do not know that our pleasure in the charms of
the loved object will disappear after possession. Even our own experience of
similar cases cannot teach us anything: when we feel a very strong stimulation
of the senses, we promise ourselves an unending happiness yet again, and then
after possession experience our error.

(2) When a person is sympathetic to us, that is, when the sound of her voice,
her way of speaking, of looking, smiling, moving, and coming and going, in
short, when all the expressions of her being enchant us and awaken in us a
nostalgic longing to sense her presence eternally—this love can perhaps survive possession, but never habit. At the beginning, we promise ourselves an
eternal, ecstatic happiness beyond any other, without ever thinking of the
power of habit. Gradually, however, habit makes itself felt: what once enchanted
us no longer does so. When we compare how the mere thought of her presence once enraptured us with the indifference it now has for us, we sense this
destruction of the feeling of joyful happiness by everyday life as a bitter disillusionment.

By good form or manners is understood the manners of a country's
upper society.

Good manners are very strictly observed—whatever their origin may be, and
whether they are rational or irrational—for they are just the signs of recognition of good society (i.e., a society superior to the crowd in the respect it enjoys) to which people want to belong at any price. Good manners are observed

most anxiously by those who are on the borderline between the elegant world and of the non-elegant world. For every fault in etiquette seems to say that they do not belong to the elegant world.

When a man of high birth does not make the bourgeois with whom he is dealing feel the superiority of his position ("he is not at all proud of his nobility"), these bourgeois appreciate the fact that he does not wound their vanity more than all the virtues he may have, and they pardon all his faults.

When one asks someone for something, one must not say (as is commonly done) "It is only a small thing," but rather "It is certainly a lot to ask." The person one is asking will give more readily if he has the prospect of being admired for his generosity.

"Having whims" does not consist in changing one's moods but in the satisfaction of making oneself and others feel the power one has over them, sometimes charming them by one's friendliness, sometimes annoying them by one's coldness, or sometimes frightening them by one's irritability.

Finally, what follows is also based on the fact that the feeling of being more prominent and distinguished than others, of being superior to them, is pleasant by itself, while the feeling of being inferior to others is painful by itself.

In the case of games, such as chess, winning is pleasant by itself; for it provides a feeling of superiority over one's opponent. In our social life, our home and dress, what we consider first of all is not our well-being but the opinion of the world: we want all this to be more elegant and better than that of others, or at least just as elegant and good as theirs. Orders and titles give us pleasure as something that distinguishes us from others. We obtain more from generosity than by force, because others do not want to acknowledge our superiority when it expresses itself in force and therefore do not do what is asked. Our own intelligence and that of our children gives us pleasure less because it brings advantages than because it distinguishes us from others. Many characters in drama act out of vanity, for example, out of a desire for power, like Wallenstein, Richard III, and the King in *Hamlet* (this desire for power is the wish to be the most prominent member of a family, party, or state); Valentin out of fury over the shame of being the brother of a dishonored girl; Don Diego in Corneille's *Cid* out of anger at having received a slap in the face (one ordinarily slaps only those who are far beneath one, such as one's valet, one's horse, or one's dog, and so to slap one's equal is a great offence, a degradation for them). Leonore Sanvitale says:

> Only then are you worthy of being envied:
> Not only do you have what many crave,
> But everyone knows and recognizes
> What it is you have! Your Fatherland
> speaks of you and looks up to you, you stand
> On the highest pinnacle of happiness![28]

Whenever someone has a new thought, his colleagues claim the thought is old (dispute over priority). We are more envious of the distinction that the qualities of others (intelligence, beauty, appearance) provide than of their usefulness. It is easier to forgive a great offence than a small one: for in the first case, one can play a role of magnanimity. It is painful when others also acquire clothing, an animal, a position, or a quality through which we ourselves are distinguished, because we have now ceased to be superior to them. Whenever someone begins to explain something to us, we are usually alarmed, for two reasons: because we are not inclined to think; and because we prefer to perform an action ourselves, rather than have it performed on us. Many young women become engaged in order to annoy their lady friends by the announcement of their engagement. We must avoid regarding someone whose favor we want to retain as cowardly, ignorant, stupid, or contemptible: for he will not forgive us. Nearly all moral failings have some aspect through which one can gain fame and distinction. For example, great over-indulgences involve physical strength. Stupidity, on the other hand, has no such compensations. Thus, many are willing to be regarded as wicked, but nobody as stupid. We always want to be in the right when we enter into a debate, above all when other people are present; each wants to show his superiority over the others. If one cannot do this by words, one tries it by blows, and then the other offers a contrary proof of his superiority by using a knife. So it is that an argument about the emperor's beard can end in a killing.

As one can see, the importance we accord to public opinion by itself (the desire to please or be distinguished over others, the fear of displeasing or being inferior to others) has a very wide influence on our occupations, our social relations, our talk, our homes, and our clothing. Indeed, even the liveliest imagination could form only an imperfect picture of what human society would be if vanity were to disappear.

If we balance up its useful and its harmful influence, we come to this conclusion:

(1) Vanity is harmful to the vain person himself in that it often brings him feelings of displeasure—on the one hand, when he displeases instead of pleasing, encounters indifference instead of admiration, or is disdained, despised, and scorned; and on the other hand, when he imposes constraints on his own well-being to avoid disapproval, indifference, or contempt, or labors out of ambition.

Vanity is useful to him in that it provides a feeling of pleasure every time he pleases or is admired or envied. (Admiration must be rare, for it depends on the great number of those who make it possible by being inferior to the admired person.) Also, the ambitious person is protected from boredom by his labors. (The sense of honor brings only feelings of displeasure and the pain of dishonor.)

(2) The vain person is harmful to his fellows. For vanity gives rise to rivalry, envy, pleasure in others' misfortune, and vengefulness. Also, the vain person presents himself as better than he is.

On the other hand, the vain person is also useful to his fellows. For in order to distinguish himself, he must accomplish things (for example, as a soldier, official, or businessman). These are just what others then strive to surpass, and so on. It is only thanks to this continual surpassing that industry, science, and the arts have come to develop; without the existence of vanity, they would still be in the cradle. Furthermore, the sense of honor prevents crime, since the disgrace attached to punishment is feared. If vanity did not exist, if punishment alone were feared and not the disgrace of punishment, its power of deterrence would probably not be great enough to maintain peace within a state. In addition, even the ruling figures would govern badly, or not govern at all, if their sense of honor were to disappear. We can thus pay homage to vanity as the protector of the state.

CHAPTER 6

Moral Progress

Moral progress occurs when people become better, that is, less egoistic, in the course of time. This can happen in two ways: through natural selection, that is, through the survival (in the struggle for existence) and reproduction of those individuals who are the most non-egoistic, or of those tribes that contain the greatest number of non-egoistic individuals; or through the frequent experience of non-egoistic feelings and frequent performance of non-egoistic actions.

(1) *Natural selection.* It is self-evident that non-egoistic individuals have no prospect of leaving behind more descendants than egoistic individuals. It only remains to consider whether the peoples whose members are relatively non-egoistic (have a strong patriotism) are always conquerors of the peoples whose members are relatively egoistic (have a weak patriotism).

First of all, when the members of a tribe of *animals* have a relatively strong social instinct, the stronger cohesion—caring and fighting for one another—that this provides gives this tribe an immense superiority in conflict with other tribes. One can hardly imagine any qualities that could replace the absence or weakness of this instinct in the tribe. Consequently, in conflicts among animal tribes, it is always the least egoistic that survive.

With human beings, however, patriotism is not so essential for the dominance of one people over others. For what matters most there is which of the peoples in conflict has the higher culture. The development of this does not depend at all on love of one's neighbor, but above all on ambition, as we have already said: all industries and sciences are promoted by the fact that everyone wants to know, be able, have, be more than others. Apart from the advantage in intellectual development, weapons, and discipline thus gained by ambitious peoples over less ambitious ones, it is particularly decisive for the outcome of a conflict which people has the best leadership, the greatest body of troops, or the strongest religious fanaticism. In fact, it is such circumstances that almost always decide the outcome; in contrast, it is only in isolated cases that the greater intensity of patriotism turns the scale, and it is hard to accept that in the future those other factors will be less decisive, and patriotism more decisive, for the victory of a people than before.

Let us add in passing that patriotism is not very strong in human beings in any case. Few persons are really prepared to sacrifice their fortune or their blood for their country. Rather, if one examines the motives from which the soldiers of an army act, one finds, with the officers in particular, ambition (a desire for distinction) and with the common soldiers, the sense of honor (fear of shame). Even with the Romans, most of the actions useful to the nation rested not on the presence of an especially strong patriotism, as is commonly supposed but on the fact that great honor was associated with just such actions, and great dishonor with contrary actions. But selflessness and patriotism are no longer so necessary even in war, now that ambition and the sense of honor render just as good service; non-egoistic feelings are important only for the harmony of the people among themselves.* For just this reason, then, it is not selfless dedication that ordinarily gains the decision in conflicts between peoples, and it is not therefore the most selfless peoples who are victorious and survive. Hence, no furthering of non-egoistic feeling can be brought about by natural selection.

In addition, in modern times the annihilation of a vanquished people does not occur.

(2) *Habit.* Every instinct or drive is reinforced by being exercised frequently. Anyone who works for others for their sake throughout his whole life will thereby acquire a stronger sense of compassion and sympathy with the joy of others and will pass on this higher degree of non-egoistic feeling to his descendants. Now, human beings no doubt continually work for others—but not for their own sake: the artisan, the peasant, the physician, the scholar, the official, the soldier perform actions useful to others not for the sake of the others, but in part to gain money and in part to gain honor. However, actions the agent himself feels as having the well-being of others only as a means, and his own well-being as their end, will reinforce his egoistic drive and not his non-egoistic drive. Genuinely non-egoistic actions are performed too seldom to reinforce our non-egoistic drive, and there is no way of increasing the number of such actions. For education to achieve this, which one might perhaps imagine, is not possible. For the feelings of benevolence, compassion, and sympathetic joy on the one hand, and those of egoism, envy, and malicious pleasure on the other, are involuntary, as we have already said, and so not dependent on our will, and therefore inaccessible either to instruction or

---

* See above, p. 96.

to even to good resolutions in any direct way. Suppose that a child passes by without concern someone dying of hunger. This unconcern can have two reasons. Either the child does not know that hunger is painful; and in that case, the child can possibly be brought to take a concern by making the painfulness of hunger something that is felt, either through imagination or actual experience. In this event, however, the child does not learn compassion, or the compassion that it has is not increased; rather, its compassion is simply given the possibility of expressing itself: even the most compassionate person can feel compassion only when he is aware of suffering. Or else the child knows that hunger is painful and nevertheless feels only little compassion. If in this case it could be led to make a resolution to feel more sympathy, that would still be useless since, as we have seen, compassion is an involuntary feeling. Hence, only an indirect influence can be envisaged: that is, by offering the child frequent opportunities to experience feelings of benevolence, compassion, and sympathetic joy, and by avoiding any opportunities to experience feelings of envy and malicious pleasure. But it is not in the power of education to control every accidental cause, and especially to protect the child from bad feelings such as envy and malicious pleasure. In reality, even the educator does not set out to produce non-egoistic feelings and actions at all; instead, he uses the hope of earthly or heavenly rewards to encourage his pupils to actions that are useful to others, or relies on the fear of punishment and shame to deter them from actions harmful to themselves and others.

Thus, as non-egoistic feelings and behavior cannot be reinforced either by natural selection (for the peoples who survive are not those who contain the greatest number of selfless individuals) or by habit (for selfless actions are very few, and their number cannot be increased at will), it is probable that human beings will always remain as selfish and envious as they are today.

Yet there certainly does exist a progress that many would describe as moral progress. That is:

(1) With uncivilized peoples, the drive to care for one's fellows relates only to members of the same tribe; every other tribe is considered as an enemy, so that the concepts of stranger and enemy are synonyms for them, and nobody wins respect unless he has killed a large number of members of enemy tribes.

A very strong trace of this view is preserved in our national rivalries. Indeed, our patriotism itself consists less in love of our own people than in hatred of rival peoples. Yet some progress in this domain has taken place: a civilized people no longer considers all other people as its enemies without further ado.

(2) Morals are variable. By good morals are understood primarily those that are profitable to the agent, such as simplicity and moderation in one's mode of life; whereas extravagance and debauchery are called bad morals because

of their harmfulness. There is no continual progress here either in the good or the bad direction: but when a people is rich and believes itself to be secure against its external enemies, and it sees self-indulgent behavior in the persons who set its tone, then it too will give itself over to self-indulgent behavior. When a people is poor or oppressed, or regards self-indulgent behavior as shameful, good morals will dominate.

Furthermore, it is morals profitable to others that are called good. As we have already said, human beings are by nature inclined to harm others for their own advantage or for the satisfaction of their vanity. When a strong government is in control, people are forced to show themselves as they are not by nature: punishment and shame prevent them from following hostile passions. Indeed, when the people who set the tone are or seem to be noble, when they make great sacrifices for their country, whether out of patriotism or to be admired, like Brutus who executed his own sons for the sake of his country, these persons will establish the fashion or custom of seeming ready to make sacrifices ("tout se conforme aux moeurs du maître").[29] The others, whether they are ready to make sacrifices or not, will endure hardships, suffering, even death itself for the sake of their country. For if they acted differently, shame would fall on them. By "good morals" is meant morals by which punishment and shame fall on every offence or lapse in duty. When there is a weak government or none at all, however, people show themselves himself as they are: they follow their passions, for punishment and shame no longer fall upon an offence. Such a state of affairs is called "bad morals."

Thus, the degree of egoistic feeling is much the same with all peoples and at all times. But where morals are good owing to the strict laws and noble or seemingly noble persons, and when following one's egoism without reserve is considered as punishable and shameful, egoism is controlled. Where morals are bad, where behaving in an absolutely egoistic way is not considered as punishable and shameful, egoism is no longer constrained. Thus, if it were possible at a given moment to eliminate the fear of punishment and fear of shame from everyone, those who have a good moral character (i.e., those who have so far imposed constraints on themselves) would behave just as badly as those who have a bad moral character: they too would satisfy their egoism without reserve. One need only observe the feelings and motives of even those who have the best moral character: if each one gazes into himself, he will find a wild beast there.

These morals too involve no continual progress: rather, when a number of strong governments chance to follow one another, when the persons upon whom the rest model their behavior are good, either genuinely or in appearance, morals are also good. When governments are weak, when the persons who set the tone are bad or do not hide their badness, morals are also bad.

(3) Human beings become more domesticated with time. The control and repression of an instinct requires the tensing of certain nerves and muscles on each occasion, and this tensing works better the more frequently it occurs, so that one is more capable of constraining the same passion the tenth time than the first time. The fluid of the nerves opens, so to speak, a path through which it can run more easily the more often it has done so. Lamarck says, "Every action is caused by some movement in the fluid of the nerves. Now when this action has been several times repeated there is no doubt that the fluid cuts a route which becomes specially easy for it to traverse, and that it acquires a readiness to follow this route in preference to others."[30] Basing himself on Johannes Müller, Darwin says the same thing in his work *The Expression of the Emotions in Man and Animals.*[31]

Since the state and society demand control of the passions, people become more capable of this in the course of time, as we have said, all the more since modifications to nerves and muscles are passed on to their descendants, so that later generations are more capable of controlling themselves than earlier ones, even from birth onward.

CHAPTER 7

The Relation of Goodness to Happiness

By a "good person" is meant, as we have already explained, the one who takes a non-egoistic, unselfish interest in the fate of others.

The question now arises whether this character is a source of happiness for the person who has it; whether the good person has a prospect of gaining happiness through his goodness.

In answering this question, it clearly depends on whether those in whose fate the good person is interested are happy or unhappy: if they are happy, his own happiness will grow through his interest in their fate, through his sympathetic joy—in that case, being good is a pleasure; on the other hand, if they are unhappy and, what is more, the good person cannot assist them, his own suffering will grow through his interest in their unhappiness, through his compassion—in that case, being good is a torment.

So let us start by trying to establish, as far as we can in general terms, whether human beings are happy or unhappy.

Nearly every person, if we observe him at a particular moment of his life, is found occupied with satisfying one of his instincts, either his self-interest (greed) or his sexual drive or his ambition (desire for fame, riches, and respect). This striving itself and the labors associated with it are felt as pain. If he actually achieves the desired object, he does not feel permanently happy through its possession; instead, as soon as he has it, it appears to him unsatisfying, indeed worthless (this is why the only love that lasts is unhappy love). Hence, either he will set himself to work toward some other goal, only to be disillusioned again when it is reached, or else he will find nothing more that seems to him worthy of striving and working for. In that case, he will be overcome by that unbearable sense of emptiness, of satiety, which is at first the cause of boredom, and then its effect.

Compared to this state of boredom, painful labor represents by far the more bearable situation. As the Bible scornfully comments about life, "its pride is only toil and trouble."[32] The only choice remaining for us is between the bearable suffering of painful labor and the unbearable suffering of boredom.

Above all, compared with other creatures, human beings are the most unhappy. The human body has the most complex nervous system and is therefore the most sensitive to pain. Occasions for this pain are found not solely in the present, as with animals, but in the past, present, and future, so that in almost every moment people are filled with cares about the future or regrets about the past. Due to its great complexity, something is usually out of order in the human organism, causing pain. We are afraid of death and yet continually get closer to it.

Human beings certainly feel not only suffering but also happiness more strongly than any other creature. But that is of no use, since we get to enjoy only very little happiness. For most people, life grants happiness only in those moments when an object one has striven for is gained: achieving the longed-for possession of a woman, a fortune, or a position gives pleasure; yet what is achieved soon loses its appeal. The more long-lasting pleasures that still exist apart from these fleeting ones, namely, intellectual pleasures, are unavailable to most people by reason of their intellectual natures, as we have already said.

What follows from this fact that human life is over-rich in feelings of displeasure and poor in sensations of pleasure is that the good person who takes a selfless interest in the fate of his fellows will have many sufferings and few joys from this interest. He will commonly feel compassion without being able to help and seldom have an occasion for sympathetic joy. The better he is, that is, the greater the number of those whose fate he takes an interest in, and the more intense this interest is, the more suffering he draws upon himself out of compassion.

The bad person, in contrast, takes no interest in the sufferings and joys of others. Their suffering does not arouse his compassion, nor their joys his own joy. From this it is now evident that, since human suffering greatly outweighs human happiness, as we have already said, the bad person is better off than the good one.

While some happiness may from time to time be granted to the good person, the bad one is not without compensation. For the pleasure the good person takes in helping his friends is no greater than the pleasure the bad one takes in harming his enemies.

Certainly on one point the bad person is at a disadvantage compared to the good one: he is sometimes overtaken by remorse. This is truly a tormenting feeling, above all when it is linked with a superstitious fear of retribution in the hereafter.

It is therefore hard to decide whether goodness brings more suffering than wickedness. The latter leads to remorse, the former to compassion that cannot come to the help of others. Both of these feelings provide very little pleasure.

If we set aside these general considerations and look at actual life, we find that goodness and badness, as they are usually distributed in human nature, normally have little influence on the happiness of the individuals in question: our goodness is not so great that we often have to be troubled by a deep compassion. Our badness does sometimes inspire us with remorse, but this is only rarely the main source of our unhappiness: whether our temperament is cheerful or melancholy, whether our passions are relatively controlled by reason or, uncontrolled, induce us to destructive excesses; whether our health is good or bad—these and other things ordinarily determine our happiness much more than the degree of our goodness or badness.

As a comment on the widespread view that virtue and happiness are related as cause to effect, we note the following:

(1) Good actions are accompanied by pleasant feelings (see chapter 1). But here one may recall that the good person pays a high price for these pleasant feelings, namely, the painful feeling of compassion in the many cases where he cannot help others.

(2) Although the term "good person" is applied only to the selfless person, the word "virtue" is applied not only to the good man in contrast with the bad one but also to the rational (moderate and consistent) person in contrast with the irrational one. Rationality, however, is actually not without importance for our happiness.

REVIEW AND CONCLUSION

When we examine our moral sense, we find that we praise as a good person someone who refrains from harming others or takes care of them out of benevolence, while we condemn as a bad person anyone who does harm to others out of selfishness or vanity (e.g., a desire for vengeance). In addition, we describe as irrational (weaknesses, errors, vices) those qualities and drives that are harmful to those who possess them.

These moral distinctions are a product of habit, that is, of the lessons and impressions felt from childhood onward. No doubt things do not seem this way to people, in part because, precisely out of habit, they feel these distinctions so strongly that they take them to be innate, and in part too because they have an interest in not attributing moral feelings to habit. For that would give them the impression that the ground is starting to move under their feet, that they are losing all support for their own behavior and for judgments on the actions of others. However true that may be, if one considers the diversity of moral distinctions among different peoples, and if one also reflects that a concept that is genuinely innate (for example, the concept of causality) presents itself as necessary and universally valid, so that we are not even capable of imagining its contrary (an effect without a cause), whereas we are perfectly capable of imagining the contrary of the moral distinctions made by us (e.g., praise of selfishness), then it emerges that moral praise and moral blame are not innate but products of habit.

The reason why non-egoism was originally called good may be found in the following. If human beings were already so non-egoistic by nature that the well-being of their fellows were as close to their heart as their own well-being, then non-egoism would never have been held up as good, as what must be done: everyone would already have been acting non-egoistically of their own accord. It is because people are instead so egoistic by nature that, for the most part, the well-being of others does not matter much to them, and because this situation results in human relations that are disharmonious and thus harmful that non-egoistic behavior, in contrast with egoism, is described as desirable, praiseworthy, and good.

Of course, this origin of the praise of non-egoism was later forgotten. For once non-egoism had come to be described as praiseworthy, this praiseworthiness itself was passed on, but not the original reason for the praise. So non-egoism has been presented to us from childhood on simply as good and egoism as bad, but we have never been told that non-egoism was originally called good because it was good for others, and egoism (e.g., cruel behavior) was originally called bad because it was bad for others. Hence, there arises in us the belief that non-egoism is good in itself, not just insofar as it is good for others, and that egoism is bad in itself, not just insofar as it is bad for others.

Further, the cause of the blame attached to qualities and instincts that are harmful not to others but to those who possess them is this harmfulness itself. So a strong attachment to sensual pleasures is condemned: because they lead to disillusionment, because they promise more than they hold, and, above all, because they last only for a short time. (If our nervous system were constructed so that sensual pleasures were by nature lasting, nobody would blame us for an attachment to them. It is solely because a lasting happiness cannot be built on them, as we have said, whereas with intellectual pleasures, in contrast, a moment of enjoyment is not paid for beforehand by unsatisfied desire or afterward by a feeling of emptiness; rather, a lasting happiness can be found in contemplation—it is for this reason alone that intellectual pleasures have been praised in preference to sensual ones.) In the same way as a strong attachment to sensuality, so too greed, intemperance, and indiscipline are condemned as qualities harmful (giving displeasure) to those who possess them. Generally one will not find any vice that was not originally called a vice and condemned as such other than because it is harmful to ourselves and others, nor any virtue that was not originally called a virtue and praised other than because it is useful to ourselves and others—although this origin of praise and blame has been lost in the course of time for some virtues and vices, just as for the good and selfless and for the bad and selfish.

If, then, the selfless person was originally called good because he is good for others, and the selfish person, for example, one who is cruel, was called bad because he is bad for others, and if the irrational person, for example one who is intemperate, was condemned (called dissolute and immoral) because his behavior harms himself, it follows that it is senseless to call selfless, cruel, or intemperate people, taken by themselves, good and bad respectively—just as it is senseless to call a moderate temperature or anything else that is good (or bad) just for human beings good (or bad) taken by itself. Taken by itself, a moderate temperature is neither good nor bad, but just a temperature of a certain nature; and similarly selfless, cruel, and intemperate persons, taken by themselves, are neither good nor bad, but just persons of a certain nature.

Yet because most people do not understand this, but consider actions such as murder to be bad and blameworthy by themselves, and because they hold the human will to be free as well, they hold themselves and others responsible for such actions. What we call remorse is this holding oneself responsible, the situation in which someone appears bad and blameworthy to himself because he has performed a bad and blameworthy action, although he could, as he believes, have refrained from it.

Anyone who has understood that the human will is not free, but that every action results with necessity from the thoughts and feelings present in the moment of action, whose causes can be traced step by step backward to the qualities with which someone is born and to the particular impressions that have acted upon him up to the moment of action—anyone who has understood that will not hold any others responsible. However, assuming that he regards so-called bad actions as bad in themselves, he will still appear blameworthy to himself, insofar as he has a character from which such blameworthy actions can result. In this remorse, then, what torments him is not the thought that he could have refrained from the blameworthy action: rather, he understands its necessity. But what pains and upsets him is the thought that his character is capable of such a blameworthy action and is therefore itself blameworthy.

Anyone, however, who has understood that the so-called bad actions, which are not bad taken by themselves but only actions of a certain nature, appear to him as bad in themselves simply because they have been presented to him as bad from childhood on will have remorse (the feeling of blameworthiness) only insofar as the habit of regarding those actions as bad by themselves is stronger than the reflection that they are not bad taken by themselves.

Finally, someone who has simply not become accustomed to regarding any action at all as blameworthy will not have any remorse (the feeling of his blameworthiness) after committing any action whatever.

For those who hold the human will to be free and bad actions to be bad in themselves, such actions seem to be not only blameworthy by themselves but also, in virtue of the feeling of justice, to be punishable and retributable by themselves. This feeling of justice arises in us, like all moral feelings, in the course of our life, and in the following way: the punishments of authorities and educators, even if their aim is only to deter (and bearing in mind that the human will is not free and that bad actions are not bad taken by themselves, their aim must be only to deter), seem to be retribution ("You are being punished because you did that"); and so there arises in us from childhood onward the belief that every bad action deserves retributive punishment. On the other hand, anyone who has understood that punishments exist and have the right

to exist only for the sake of deterrence will no longer want to see a criminal punished for his bad actions themselves, but solely as a means to an end, in order to deter him from bad actions for the well-being of all.

A host of other feelings can be explained by the importance placed on public opinion in itself (pleasure in pleasing and being admired, pain at displeasing and being despised). This feeling arises because pleasing and being admired and distinguished over others is felt as pleasant, at first for its useful consequences and then owing to acquired habit, in itself. In order to gain this pleasant feeling of superiority, one will, for example, put others down, above all when they think they have proven their superiority over us by inflicting some pain (desire for vengeance). In general, many feelings and situations arise out of the importance accorded to public opinion, that is, out of vanity.

Moreover, one cannot assume that people become better, that is, more non-egoistic, in the course of time: for non-egoistic individuals or peoples do not survive by natural selection; nor is non-egoistic feeling reinforced by frequent exercise. It is remarkable that people, while egoistic, selfish, and envious in their actions, should assert the reality of moral progress as soon as they themselves start to philosophize. Where could this progress come from?

In the end, our happiness depends less on whether we are egoistic or non-egoistic than on other factors such as health, temperament, and rationality.

❧

In this work, the nature and origin of the moral sensations have been presented without concern for whether reading it would be harmful or useful. Only in this way can knowledge be served: nothing can be sacred to the philosopher but truth.

Anyone, however, who dares to see only as much of the truth as is useful, or at least not harmful, will in most cases see only a little of it.

Certainly, if the moral person is higher in rank, and if the seeker of knowledge must defer to him, then one should uncover only as much of the truth as is tolerable to the moral person. The moral person, however, is not higher in rank, although most hold this to be immediately certain, for the following reasons. Disinterested knowledge of the true and the beautiful is something very recent in the development of humanity. What comes first is utility and well-being, to which morality too has contributed, as we have shown. Morality is indeed very essential to human well-being and, insofar as the good person serves the welfare of others and the bad person harms others out of selfishness or vanity, goodness is always valued more highly than anything else and has been presented to us from childhood on, as for earlier generations, as something to be valued so highly. If we reflect, however, that the non-egoistic person, since he was originally praised just for his utility, is no more to be valued than animals that have a strong social instinct (e.g., bees or ants), whereas disinterested knowledge not only is not found in animals, but rather rests on a powerful development of just those organs by which we are most distinct from the animals, namely, of the intellect, then it follows that knowledge of the true and the beautiful is higher in rank than good behavior; indeed, it is the highest thing that human beings can attain and therefore must be sought without consideration of its utility or harmfulness.

In addition, if disinterested knowledge does not make someone better or more non-egoistic directly, nevertheless a certain utility is indirectly linked with it. That is, knowledge is peaceable by its nature: everyone can devote themselves to knowledge of the same thing without feeling rivalry or hostility. But desire is always warlike: two people cannot desire the same thing without feeling mutual hostility. Hence, the writings and works of art that inspire one to knowledge of the true and beautiful, although otherwise useless, have the utility of leading people away from activities arousing hostility (owing to desire) to peaceful activities, as far as the intellectual nature of each permits.

In addition, every desire is itself painful, even for the desiring person himself, but knowledge is pleasurable.

Thus, without being useful through a direct improvement, pleasure in knowledge does rescue us from desires that are painful and create hostility, and so it is useful to this extent.

NOTES

1. Helvétius, *Treatise on Man*, 1:126.

2. Hutcheson, *System of Moral Philosophy*, book 1, chap. 3, in *Collected Works*, 5:38–52.

3. Hume, *Enquiry concerning the Principles of Morals*, app. 2, in *Enquiries*, 302. The original text reads: "Now where is the difficulty in conceiving that this may likewise be the case with benevolence and friendship, and that, from the original frame of our temper, we may feel a desire of another's happiness or good, which, by means of that affection, becomes our own good, and is afterwards pursued from the combined motives of benevolence and self-enjoyments?"

4. Schopenhauer, *Kleinere Schriften*, 404. The passage from Copernicus's *De Revolutionibus*, 1.9, quoted here begins: "Equidem existimo gravitatem non aliud esse quam appetentiam quandam naturalem partibus inditam a divina providentia opificis universorum, ut in unitatem integritatemque suam se conferant in formam globi coeuntes."

5. Brehm, *Illustriertes Thierleben*, 1:25.

6. Lubbock, *Origin of Civilisation*, 322.

7. Mill, *System of Logic*, book 2, chap. 5, sect. 6, p. 157.

8. Hume typically says: "The hypothesis which we embrace is plain. It maintains that morality is determined by sentiment. It defines virtue to be whatever mental action or quality gives to a spectator the pleasing sentiment of approbation." *Enquiry concerning the Principles of Morals*, app. 1, in *Enquiries*, 289.

9. Kant, *Critique of Practical Reason*, part 1, book 1, chap. 3, p. 103.

10. Seneca, "On Anger," book 19, 10–11. Rée refers to Seneca's "Num, ut Plato ait, nemo prudens punit, quia peccatum est, sed ne peccetur": "For, as Plato says, 'A sensible person does not punish a man because he has sinned, but in order to keep him from sin.'" Seneca, *Moral Essays*, 1:158–59; see Plato, *Laws*, book 11, 934, in *Dialogues*, 2:672.

11. See the previous note.

12. Hobbes, *Leviathan*, chap. 28: "Poena malum est transgressori legis auctoritate publica inflictum, eo fine, ut terrore ejus voluntas civium ad obedientam conformetur." Rée cites Hobbes's own Latin translation of the following passage: "A punishment, is an Evill inflicted by publique Authority, on him that hath done, or omitted that which is Judged by the same Authority to be a Transgression of the Law; to the end that the will of men may thereby the better be disposed to obedience."

13. Plato, *Protagoras*, 324, in *Dialogues*, 1:95.

14. Plato, *Laws*, book 5, 736: "When men who have nothing, and are in want of food, show a disposition to follow their leaders in an attack on the property of the rich—

these, who are the natural plague of the state, are sent away by the legislator in a friendly spirit as far as he is able; and this dismissal of them is euphemistically called a colony." *Dialogues*, 2:503.

15. Locke, *Essay concerning Human Understanding*, 1:105.

16. Helmholtz, *Treatise on Physiological Optics*, 3:21–22.

17. Spinoza, *Ethics*, app. to part 1: "Videmus omnes notiones, quibus vulgus solet naturam explicare [i.e., bonum et malum, ordinem, confusionem, calidium, frigidium, pulchritudinem et deformitatem, etc.] modos esse tantummodo imaginandi nec ullius rei naturam, sed tantum imaginationis constitutionem indicare." *Opera*, 2:83. The words in brackets were added by Rée.

18. Ibid., preface to part 4: "Bonum et malum, quod attinet, nihil etiam positivum in rebus, in se scilicet consideratis, indicant, nec aliud sunt praeter cogitandi modos seu notiones." *Opera*, 2:208.

19. See Tylor, *Primitive Culture*, 1:397–402, and Lubbock, *Origin of Civilisation*, 126–27.

20. Rée's discussion here is based on Darwin, *The Descent of Man, and Selection in Relation to Sex*, chaps. 13–14, in *Works*, vol. 22, see esp. 382–89 and 408.

21. Darwin, *Variation of Animals and Plants under Domestication*, in *Works*, vols. 19–20.

22. Schopenhauer, *On the Basis of Morality*, sect. 14, 132.

23. Cf. sect. 88 of *Psychological Observations*.

24. Rée is here citing a German proverb: "Wer den Schaden hat, braucht für den Spott nicht zu sorgen."

25. *Socios habuisse malorum*: "having companions in misfortune." Cf. sect. 452 of *Psychological Observations*.

26. Cf. sect. 117 of *Psychological Observations*.

27. The theory criticized here was championed by Eugen Dühring in various writings; see, e.g., *Der Werth des Lebens*, 20–21.

28. Goethe, *Torquato Tasso*, act 3, scene 3, line 86.

29. *Tout se conforme aux moeurs du maître*: "everything conforms to the master's manners."

30. Lamarck, *Zoological Philosophy*, part 3, chap. 5, 349–50.

31. Darwin quotes Müller's statement (in his *Elements of Physiology*) "that the conducting power of the nervous fibres increases with the frequency of their excitement." *The Expression of the Emotions in Man and Animals*, chap. 1, in *Works*, 23:21.

32. Psalm 90:10. Rée cites Martin Luther's German translation: "Wenn es köstlich gewesen ist, so ist es Mühe und Arbeit gewesen."

BIBLIOGRAPHY

WORKS OF PAUL RÉE

Psychologische Beobachtungen: Aus dem Nachlass von *₊*. Berlin: Carl Duncker, 1875.
Der Ursprung der moralischen Empfindungen. Chemnitz: Ernst Schmeitzner, 1877.
Die Illusion der Willensfreiheit, ihre Ursachen und ihren Folgen. Berlin: Carl Duncker, 1885.
Die Entstehung des Gewissens. Berlin: Carl Duncker, 1885.
Philosophie (Nachgelassenes Werk). Berlin: Carl Duncker, 1903.

SECONDARY LITERATURE

Alexander, Richard D. *Darwinism and Human Affairs*. Seattle: University of Washington Press, 1979.
Allison, David B. *Reading the New Nietzsche*. Lanham, Md.: Rowman and Littlefield, 2001.
Andler, Charles. *Nietzsche, sa vie et sa pensée*. 6 vols. Paris: Gallimard, 1923–58.
Andreas-Salomé, Lou. *Looking Back: Memoirs*. Trans. Breon Mitchell. Ed. Ernst Pfeiffer. New York: Paragon House, 1990.
Aristotle. *The Basic Works of Aristotle*. Ed. Richard McKeon. New York: Random House, 1941.
Assoun, Paul-Laurent. "Nietzsche et le Réealisme." In Paul Rée, *De l'origine des sentiments moraux*. Trans. Michel-François Demet. 5–68. Paris: Presses Universitaires de France, 1982.
Axelrod, Robert. *The Evolution of Co-operation*. Harmondsworth, England: Penguin, 1984.
Axelrod, Robert, and William D. Hamilton. "The Evolution of Cooperation." *Science* 211, no. 4489 (Mar. 27, 1981): 1390–96.
Babich, Babette E. *Nietzsche's Philosophy of Science: Reflecting Science on the Ground of Art and Life*. Albany: State University of New York Press, 1994.
Bain, Alexander. *Mental and Moral Science, Part Second: Theory of Ethics and Ethical Systems*. London: Longmans, Green, 1884.
Binion, Rudolf. *Frau Lou: Nietzsche's Wayward Disciple*. Princeton: Princeton University Press, 1968.
Brehm, Alfred Edmund. *Illustriertes Thierleben: Eine allgemeine Kunde des Thierreichs*. 6 vols. Hildburghausen, Germany: Verlag des Bibliographischen Instituts, 1864–69.

Chamfort, Sébastien Roch Nicolas de. *Products of the Perfected Civilization: Selected Writings of Chamfort.* Trans. W. S. Merwin. New York: Macmillan, 1969.

Darwin, Charles. *The Works of Charles Darwin.* 29 vols. Ed. Paul H. Barrett and R. B. Freeman. London: William Pickering, 1986–89.

Dennett, Daniel C. *Darwin's Dangerous Idea: Evolution and the Meanings of Life.* Harmondsworth, England: Penguin, 1995.

Diethe, Carol. *Nietzsche's Women: Beyond the Whip.* Berlin: Walter de Gruyter, 1996.

Donnellan, Brendan. "Friedrich Nietzsche and Paul Rée: Co-operation and Conflict." *Journal of the History of Ideas* 43, no. 4 (Oct. 1982): 595–612.

Dühring, Eugen. *Robert Mayer der Galilei des neunzehnten Jahrhunderts.* Chemnitz, Germany: Ernst Schmeitzner, 1880.

———. *Der Werth des Lebens: Eine philosophische Betrachtung.* Breslau, Germany: Eduard Trewendt, 1865.

Feuerbach, Paul Johann Anselm. *Revision der Grundsätze und Grundbegriffe des positiven peinlichen Rechts.* 2 vols. Erfurt, Germany: in der Henningschen Buchhandlung, 1799–1800.

Förster-Nietzsche, Elisabeth. *The Lonely Nietzsche.* Trans. Paul V. Cohn. New York: Sturgis and Walton, 1915.

Gayon, Jean. "Nietzsche and Darwin." In Jane Maienschein and Michael Ruse, eds., *Biology and the Foundation of Ethics.* 154–97. Cambridge: Cambridge University Press, 1999.

Goethe, Johann Wolfgang von. *Torquato Tasso.* Trans. A. Brownjohn and S. Brownjohn. London: Angel Books, 1985.

Hamilton, William D. "The Evolution of Altruistic Behavior." *American Naturalist* 97, no. 896 (Sept.–Oct. 1963): 354–56.

Hayman, Ronald. *Nietzsche: A Critical Life.* Harmondsworth, England: Penguin, 1980.

Helmholtz, Hermann von. *Treatise on Physiological Optics.* Trans. J. P. C. Southall. 3 vols. [Rochester, N.Y.: Optical Society of America, 19224–25.] New York: Dover, 1962.

Helvétius, Claude-Adrien. *A Treatise on Man.* Trans. W. Hooper. 2 vols. [London: James Cundee, 1810.] New York: Burt Franklin, 1969.

Hobbes, Thomas. *The English Works of Thomas Hobbes.* Ed. W. Molesworth. 11 vols. London: J. Bohn, 1839–45.

———. *Opera philosophica quae Latine scripsit omnia.* Ed. W. Molesworth. 5 vols. London: J. Bohn, 1839–45.

Hollingdale, R. J. *Nietzsche: The Man and His Philosophy.* 2d ed. Cambridge: Cambridge University Press, 2001.

Hume, David. *Enquiries concerning the Human Understanding and concerning the Principles of Morals.* Ed. L. A. Selby-Bigge. 2d ed. Oxford: Clarendon Press, 1902.

Hutcheson, Francis. *Collected Works of Francis Hutcheson.* [Glasgow: Robert Foulis, 1755.] 7 vols. Hildesheim: Georg Olms, 1969.

Janz, Curt Paul. *Friedrich Nietzsche Biographie.* 3 vols. Munich: Deutsche Taschenbuch Verlag, 1981.

Jaspers, Karl. *Nietzsche: Einführung in das Verständnis seines Philosophierens.* 3d ed. Berlin: Walter de Gruyter, 1950.

Kant, Immanuel. *Critique of Practical Reason.* Trans. L. W. Beck. Indianapolis: Bobbs-Merrill, 1956.

Kolle, Kurt. "Notizen über Paul Rée." *Zeitschrift für Menschenkunde und Zentralblatt für Graphologie* 3 (Sept. 1927): 168–74.

Lamarck, J. B. *Zoological Philosophy.* Trans. H. Elliot. [London: Macmillan, 1914.] New York: Hafner, 1963.

La Rochefoucauld, François, duc de. *Maxims.* Trans. L. W. Tancock. Harmondsworth, England: Penguin, 1959.

Locke, John. *An Essay concerning Human Understanding.* Ed. John W. Yolton. Rev. ed. 2 vols. London: Dent, 1965.

Lubbock, Sir John. *The Origin of Civilisation and the Primitive Condition of Man: Mental and Social Conditions of Savages.* London: Longmans, Green, 1870.

Lucretius. *De rerum natura.* Trans. W. H. D. Rouse. Rev. M. F. Smith. Loeb Classical Library. Cambridge, Mass.: Harvard University Press, 1975.

Maynard Smith, John. "The Evolution of Behavior." *Scientific American* 239, no. 3 (Sept. 1978): 136–45.

Meysenbug, Malwida von. *Individualitäten.* 2d ed. Berlin: Schuster and Loeffler, 1902.

———. *Memoiren einer Idealistin.* 3 vols. Berlin: Schuster and Loeffler, 1903.

Mill, John Stuart. *A System of Logic.* 8th ed. London: Longmans, 1970.

Molière. *Oeuvres complètes.* Ed. Georges Couton. Bibliothèque de la Pléiade. 2 vols. Paris: Gallimard, 1971.

Moore, Gregory. *Nietzsche, Biology, and Metaphor.* Cambridge: Cambridge University Press, 2002.

Morawski, Charlotte. *Der Einfluss Rées auf Nietzsches neue Moralideen.* Breslau, Germany: Druck von Gottl. Korn, 1915.

Nietzsche, Friedrich. *Basic Writings of Nietzsche.* Trans. and ed. Walter Kaufmann. New York: Modern Library, 1966.

———. *Daybreak: Thoughts on the Prejudices of Morality.* Trans. R. J. Hollingdale. Cambridge: Cambridge University Press, 1982.

———. *The Gay Science.* Trans. Walter Kaufmann. New York: Random House, 1974.

———. *Human, All-Too-Human: A Book For Free Spirits.* Trans. R. J. Hollingdale. Cambridge: Cambridge University Press, 1986.

———. *Kritische Gesamtausgabe: Briefwechsel.* Ed. Giorgio Colli and Mazzino Montinari. 24 vols. Berlin: Walter de Gruyter, 1975–84.

———. *Kritische Gesamtausgabe: Werke.* Ed. Giorgio Colli and Mazzino Montinari. 30 vols. Berlin: Walter de Gruyter, 1967–78.

———. *The Portable Nietzsche.* Trans. and ed. Walter Kaufmann. New York: Viking Press, 1954.

———. *Untimely Meditations.* Trans. R. J. Hollingdale. Cambridge: Cambridge University Press, 1983.

―――. *The Will to Power*. Trans. Walter Kaufmann and R. J. Hollingdale. Ed. Walter Kaufmann. New York: Vintage, 1968.

Plato. *The Dialogues of Plato*. Trans. B. Jowett. 2 vols. New York: Random House, 1937.

Plutarch. *Moralia*. Trans. F. C. Babbitt. Loeb Classical Library. 15 vols. Cambridge, Mass.: Harvard University Press, 1956.

Pfeiffer, Ernst. *Friedrich Nietzsche, Paul Rée, Lou von Salomé: Die Dokumente ihrer Begegnung*. Frankfurt: Insel Verlag, 1970.

Review of Paul Rée, *Der Ursprung der moralischen Empfindungen*. *Mind* 2, no. 8 (Oct. 1877): 581.

Ridley, Matt. *The Origins of Virtue*. London: Viking, 1996.

Rolph, W. H. *Biologische Probleme, zugleich als Versuch einer rationellen Ethik*. Leipzig: Wilhelm Engelmann, 1882.

Schaberg, William. *The Nietzsche Canon: A Publication History and Bibliography*. Chicago: University of Chicago Press, 1995.

Schopenhauer, Arthur. *Kleinere Schriften*. Darmstadt, Germany: Wissenschaftliche Buchgesellschaft, 1962.

―――. *On the Basis of Morality*. Trans. E. F. J. Payne. Indianapolis: Hackett, 1996.

―――. *Parerga and Paralipomena*. Trans. E. F. J. Payne. 2 vols. Oxford: Clarendon Press, 1974.

―――. *The World as Will and Representation*. Trans. E. F. J. Payne. 2 vols. New York: Peter Smith, 1969.

Seneca. *Moral Essays*. Trans. John W. Basore. Loeb Classical Library. 3 vols. London: Heinemann, 1928–35.

Small, Robin. *Nietzsche in Context*. Aldershot, England: Ashgate, 2001.

Sober, Elliott. "What Is Evolutionary Altruism?" *Canadian Journal of Philosophy* supp. vol. 14 (1988): 75–99.

Sober, Elliott, and David Sloan Wilson. *Unto Others: The Evolution and Psychology of Unselfish Behavior*. Cambridge, Mass.: Harvard University Press, 1998.

Spencer, Herbert. *The Data of Ethics*. London: Williams and Norgate, 1879.

―――. "Progress: Its Law and Cause." *Westminster Review* 11, no. 2 (Apr. 1, 1857): 445–85.

―――. *Social Statics*. London: John Chapman, 1851.

Spinoza, Benedict de. *Opera*. Ed. Carl Gebhardt. 4 vols. Heidelberg: Carl Winters, 1924.

Strong, Tracy B. *Friedrich Nietzsche and the Politics of Transfiguration*. Expanded ed. Urbana: University of Illinois Press, 2000.

Tönnies, Ferdinand. "Paul Rée." *Das Freie Wort* 4 (1904–5): 666–73.

Treiber, Hubert. "Gruppenbilder mit einer Dame." *Forum: Internationale Zeitschrift für kulturelle Freiheit politische Gleichheit und solidarische Arbeit*, no. 409–10 (Jan.–Feb. 1988): 40–54.

―――. "Nachträge zu Paul Rée." *Nietzsche-Studien* 27 (1998): 515–16.

―――. "Paul Rée—Ein Freund Nietzsches." *Bündner Jahrbuch* 29 (1987): 35–59.

―――. "Zur Genealogie einer 'science positive de la morale en Allemagne': Die Geburt der 'r(é)ealistischen Moralwissenschaft' aus der Idee einer monistischen Naturkonzeption." *Nietzsche-Studien* 22 (1993): 165–221.

Trivers, Robert L. "The Evolution of Reciprocal Altruism." *Quarterly Review of Biology* 46, no. 1 (Mar. 1971): 35–57.

Tylor, Edward B. *Primitive Culture: Researches into the Development of Mythology, Philosophy, Religion, Art, and Custom.* 2 vols. London: John Murray, 1871.

Vauvenargues, Luc de Clapiers, marquis de. *Oeuvres complètes.* Ed. Henry Bonnier. 2 vols. Paris: Hachette, 1968.

Wagner, Cosima. *Diaries.* Trans. Geoffrey Skelton. Ed. Martin Gregor-Ellin and Dietrich Mack. 2 vols. New York: Harcourt Brace Jovanovich, 1978–80.

Wagner, Richard. *Richard Wagner's Prose Works.* Trans. William Ashton Ellis. 8 vols. London: Kegan Paul, Trench, Trübner, and Co., 1897.

Wilhelmi, Johann Heinrich. *Th. Carlyle und F. Nietzsche: Wie sie Gott suchten, und was für einen Gott sie fanden.* Göttingen: Vandenhoeck und Ruprecht, 1897.

Williams, C. M. *A Review of the Systems of Ethics Founded on the Theory of Evolution.* London: Macmillan, 1893.

INDEX

INTERNATIONAL NIETZSCHE STUDIES

The University of Illinois Press
is a founding member of the
Association of American University Presses.

University of Illinois Press
1325 South Oak Street
Champaign, IL 61820-6903
www.press.uillinois.edu